Dr. Carren Marv

EXODUS

LESSONS AS YOU LEAVE

21st CENTURY CHRISTIAN

ISBN: 978-0-89098-920-3

Cover design by Jonathan Edelhuber

DEDICATION

To the FRIENDS Ministry,
who walked through deep waters with me

And to Stephen,
whose selfless, crazy love reminds me of God's

ACKNOWLEDGEMENTS

This book came about because everyone fell asleep. Everyone except me, that is. I should probably clarify that it was around 2:00am on a weeknight. My husband and children, to their credit, were preparing their bodies for a full day of work and school (as I should have been), while I was sitting upright in bed wondering who in my Contacts list wouldn't mind a call at that hour.

Negative.

With my Bible on my lap and Exodus bookmarked by my cat's lazy front paw, I contemplated what to do with this fresh insight I had about God and His redemptive plans for us. I felt the excitement of a Pentecostal preacher, yet something told me my husband wouldn't share my enthusiasm if I woke him up at that hour.

And so this book was born. I grabbed a notebook and began scribbling myself back into carpal tunnel syndrome. The process of completing this book, however, was certainly not a solo flight. I am honored and humbled by the support that has surrounded me, and I pray special blessings upon these people!

Stacey Owens, my editor and friend, you are so gifted at what you do. I am so thankful for your encouragement and affirmation.

Kelley Williams, you turned my weary heart toward Exodus several years ago. Thank you for showing me a purpose in dark times, for even encouraging me to hide "in the cleft of the rock."

Jen Farmer, you are a precious friend, and you embraced this study from the beginning. Thank you for your honest feedback.

Beth Crooks, you had a press badge to cut into many of the moments when I learned these lessons firsthand. Your grace, poise, and perseverance reassured me of His.

My parents and my sisters have been steadfast in their excitement, and they continue to dote over my writing. They think I'm a celebrity! My autograph is shaped by their love.

My boys, Drew and Jack—my love, my heart, my joy. Though they still want me to write a murder mystery, they blessed this manuscript with their brilliant minds, their infectious laughter, and their tender love.

My husband, confidante, and best buddy ever, Stephen. His wisdom keeps me grounded, even as his jokes have me doubled over laughing. His support of this manuscript took many shapes—from a midnight run to Sonic for yet another sweet tea for me, to extra housework while I was finishing up the final draft, to lengthy conversations about the truths we were learning together as I wrote on the book of Exodus. He is the gift God gave me to "restore the years that the locusts ha[d] eaten" (Joel 2:25), my strength in the journey heavenward.

TABLE OF CONTENTS

INTRODUCTION

When I was in eleventh grade, I had a hard fall one February morning as I rushed to my homeroom class. Near an outside door, the classroom required all things to be waterproof during winter months when melted snow we brought in on our shoes formed small bodies of water in random places.

I was in a hurry—I didn't want to be tardy. I speed walked through the entrance door at the end of the hall, bypassed the large and wisely placed floor mat, and slopped my snowy way to my classroom door.

I didn't make it *into* the classroom.

The snow on my shoes slapped a high-five to fellow water molecules on the floor, and I fell. Hard. Immediately embarrassed (and still worried about being tardy), I tried to get up. My body said, "No way," and I lay my head back on the slushy floor and cried.

In keeping with my tendency to overachieve, I had broken my tailbone pretty impressively. When the doctor saw the herculean size and obvious weight of the backpack I had been carrying—apparently, the school nurse thought it was wise to send it in the ambulance with me—he grimaced. "That's why you broke it so hard," he said.

I can't help but think of that experience as I read Exodus and contemplate its implications for God's church. How often do we rush through life carrying heavy, unnecessary loads? How often do we justify those loads in the name of some greater good? And, not surprisingly, how often do we fall hard and fast because of those loads, crippling us for God's service?

The nation of Israel was enslaved by the Egyptians. Bearing an impossible weight of abuse and torture, they longed for deliverance. Today, we are in danger of being enslaved by sin. Crippled by heavy loads of anxiety, fear, lust, pride, or whatever sin to which we play host, we long for deliverance. Like the Israelites who later thought they should have remained in slavery, though, we often return to the very burdens God lifted off us. We pick them up again. And we fall again under their weight.

This study is about leaving. Leaving behind sin. Leaving behind the huge burdens we carry, burdens that enslave us and keep us from God's best. If leaving were easy, however, this study would be unnecessary.

But it isn't our natural reaction to let go. You see, I still carry a behemoth bag to work, to church, to ladies' events. I still can't quite be at ease without my portable office on my shoulder. Though this tendency merely keeps my chiropractor employed, I worry that in my spiritual life I, too, return to heavy burdens—sinful habits of thinking and doing that keep me trying to enter God's rest with chains on my feet.

If you can relate, please read with me God's invitation, and let us begin our exodus together.

"Therefore, . . . let us also lay aside every weight, and sin which clings so closely" (Hebrews 12:1).

God Won't Leave You Out in the Cold
(EXODUS 1-3)

LIFE LESSON 1
Your enemy wants to destroy you.

We're going to begin this journey with a cold, hard truth: You have an enemy, and that enemy wants to ruin you completely.

As sojourners in Egypt, the Israelites were thriving despite the new Pharaoh's ever-tightening reigns. Exodus 1:9-10, 15-16, and 22 show us, however, the motive behind this pharaoh's cruelty. He aimed to annihilate the Israelites. That's right. He wasn't a randomly mean-spirited ruler who tortured everyone in sight. Nope. He saw the Israelites multiplying—a sure sign of God's blessings on them—and he panicked. Afraid they would overtake Egypt, he plotted their destruction.

Does this pattern seem familiar to you? Maybe you've experienced success, only to be undermined by a colleague. Or perhaps the victory of a few pounds you lost on your new diet was quickly zapped by a convenient fast food drive-thru. Maybe a toxic dating relationship has nearly ruined your Christian walk, or your quick temper threatens the security of all you love.

Your enemy is not an Egyptian pharaoh, and—believe it or not—it's not even liquor, an abusive lover, or a power-hungry boss. Your enemy is Satan himself. He will gladly assume the appearance of an expensive new purse, especially if buying it puts you in debt. He revels at the chance to scream fattening taunts each time your anorexic frame approaches a mirror. But make no mistake: He is after your very soul.

First Peter 5:8 confirms this, comparing Satan himself to a "roaring lion" scrounging for his lunch. Women seem to struggle with this reality, though. As women, God designed us to be nurturers, caretakers, and lovers. We quickly defend what we love, and we are gracious hosts to any substance or being that will provide even a momentary refill of the comfort we so readily spend on others. "It was just innocent flirting," a married woman might say after attending a class reunion without her husband. "Every other mom is doing it," a career mom explains as she takes on yet another volunteer task at the children's school.

And that's where we are deceived. Despite the gentle, convicting nudge of the Holy Spirit deep within us, we rationalize the welcome mat we just placed at the threshold of sin.

The devil is not satisfied with making you uncomfortable. His appetite is for your very soul, and he will eat you one bite at a time if he must. When that truth resonates within you, you can see your oppressors for what they are and begin to pack your bags for an exodus.

The Nation of Israel: Key Concepts
Read Exodus 1 as you identify these key concepts.

1. Why did the new pharaoh feel threatened by the Israelites? (Exodus 1:8-10)

2. What word does Scripture give us to describe how the Egyptians made the Israelites work? (Exodus 1:13-14)

3. What was ironic about the Israelites' growth as a nation under harsh Egyptian slavery? (Exodus 1:12)

4. Since hard labor wasn't ruining them, what was the pharaoh's plan? (Exodus 1:16 and 22; Acts 7:19)

5. What tremendous act of obedience to God saved many of the Hebrew babies? (Exodus 1:17)

_____

_____

_____

_____

_____

_____

_____

_____

Thinking it through . . .

1. What do you remember about how the Israelites initially ended up in Egypt?

2. If resettlement in Egypt was a way of saving the Israelites during a famine, then why do they end up being tortured and abused there?

3. Do modern-day nations feel threatened when other nationalities begin to grow and consume much of the population of the host country? What are your thoughts on this?

_____

_____

_____

_____

_____

_____

_____

_____

_____

The Church: Key Concepts

1. Why might Satan feel threatened by God's people here on earth? (Matthew 16:18-19; John 15:19)

2. When does Satan typically approach us? (Matthew 4:2-3a)

3. What can happen to us when we give in to temptations? (Galatians 5:1 and 6:8; James 1:15)

4. What is Satan's ultimate goal when it comes to you? (1 Peter 5:8)

5. Does God want you to live in bondage and slavery? (John 10:10; Romans 6:6-7; Hebrews 12:1)

_____

_____

_____

_____

_____

_____

_____

_____

Thinking it through . . .

1. In what ways does Satan try to ensnare you?

2. How can a good thing turn into an oppressive, sinful situation?

3. Imagine you just got a job, and the devil is your boss. What kinds of tasks would he ask you to do? Do you already do some of these tasks for him?

4. What does Jesus say about serving two masters?

5. How can your sisters in Christ support you in your exodus?

_____

_____

_____

_____

_____

_____

_____

_____

LIFE LESSON 2
God hears your groaning.

Initially, Egypt was a relief for the Israelites—a means of salvation, actually. In a miraculous turn of events years prior to Exodus, the Israelites were invited to Egypt so they could survive amidst widespread famine. The pharaoh who welcomed them was long gone, though, and the reigning pharaoh felt threatened by the presence of so many immigrants. His graduated plan of torture included backbreaking labor and cold-blooded slaughter.

Grief is likely an understatement as we try to capture the tremendous angst the Israelites felt during this time. Try to picture it: Men stumbling into their tents, dry heaving from dehydration and oozing from infectious blisters, only to behold their wives with animalistic self-inflicted wounds or impenetrable catatonic gazes resulting from that day's infant slaughtering spree. Death would be a relief to either party, yet in what may have seemed like a cruel twist of providence, they keep living and multiplying. Yet the abuse and torture continue. *Where is God?*

I don't think I will ever forget the ear-ringing vibrato of a college friend's voice as she threw herself on the dorm room floor and, gripping the phone fiercely, screamed, "*Where is God?! Where is Gooooooooooooooddd?!?!*" Her father had just been sentenced to prison for a crime he did not commit.

Maybe that's how you feel right now—imprisoned unjustly. Harassed and abused *just because* . . . well, just because. Like the Israelites, you are doing your darndest, but the oppression continues. In fact, under God's very nose, the only certainty you have is that your pain is only getting worse. *Where is God? Where is God?!?!*

The answer to that is this: right here. In fact, He is so close that He hears you crying. His heart is breaking, and, like you, He knows something must be done.

Because we are painfully human, we want relief NOW. Romans 8:25-26 is a gentle reminder, however, that we must wait patiently: "But if we hope for what we do not see, we wait for it with patience. Likewise the Spirit helps us in our weakness. For we do not know what to pray for as we ought, but the Spirit himself intercedes for us with groanings too deep for words." So what is God doing while we wait? Read verse 26 again because it says that He is praying for us "with groanings too deep for words." And who knows? He may also be safeguarding your deliverer in a wicker basket.

While you cry, He is crying with you. You groan and wail, and He does the same (John 11:35; Romans 12:15). Regardless of whether your exodus is minutes or months away, rest your weary heart on this truth: God sees you, and He knows.

The Nation of Israel: Key Concepts

Read Exodus 2 as you identify these key concepts.

1. When destruction seemed imminent, what did the Levite woman do with her three-month-old baby? (Exodus 2:3)

2. Ironically, what opportunity did the woman have soon thereafter? (Exodus 2:8-9)

3. What does the name "Moses" apparently mean? (Exodus 2:10)

4. Why did Moses kill an Egyptian? (Exodus 2:11)

5. Why did Moses go into hiding? (Exodus 2:15)

6. Where does Scripture say that the Israelites' cry for help went? (Exodus 2:23b)

7. What is God's response? (Exodus 2:24-25)

_____

_____

_____

_____

_____

_____

_____

_____

_____

Thinking it through . . .

1. What do you imagine it was like for Moses's mother to put her tiny baby in a basket and, presumably, walk away from him?

2. Why do you think God gave her the opportunity to nurse her own child?

3. Can you think of places in our modern world where groups of people live in a constant state of turmoil and/or oppression? Have you heard people use this as evidence that there must not be a God or that God is not loving and kind? What would you say to those people?

_____

_____

_____

_____

_____

_____

_____

_____

_____

The Church: Key Concepts

1. With evil present everywhere in the world, what is God's way of protecting us? (Psalm 91:1 and 4)

2. What did Jesus promise would be ours after He left the earth? (John 14:16)

3. What is the Holy Spirit doing on your behalf during your weak moments? (Romans 8:26)

_____

_____

_____

_____

_____

_____

_____

_____

_____

Thinking it through . . .

1. Some people say, "If I could just feel God or see Him, I would believe." Do you think God made a way for believers and nonbelievers to feel Him and see Him at work?

2. Why does so much suffering exist in the world?

3. Is there evidence in the world (outside of Scripture) today that God still "sees" and "knows" the pain that people face?

4. Is there an area of hurt, pain, embarrassment, shame, etc. that you are aching under right now?

5. Describe what kinds of experiences remind you that God sees you and remembers your pain.

_____

_____

_____

_____

_____

_____

_____

_____

_____

LIFE LESSON 3

God doesn't work within the limits we set for Him.

If I were to write a screenplay of the Israelites' exodus out of Egypt, Moses—a fugitive guilty of murder—wouldn't have been my pick for the ringleader. In my script, God would not have lit a match to a flimsy bush when He wanted to speak. And God's plan wouldn't have been as audacious as the enslaved Israelites' leaving royal Egypt with their Hebrew women decked out in Egyptian jewels.

In my limited point of view, I would have selected a robust, courageous warrior with a track record of victory. God would have spoken in a magnificent oration from heaven, and He would have offered a graduated plan of deliverance that simply made more sense.

At some point in your walk with Christ, you've probably struggled against your finite understanding of your potential versus God's nerve. We expect God to . . . well, *make sense.* I wonder if we miss Yahweh, the God Who is, because we are looking instead for the God we *think* He is. I wonder if He walks right by us unnoticed because we're on our tiptoes straining to hear the pomp and circumstance we think should accompany the miracle of Jesus.

We have a desperate financial need: in digging through the mailbox hungry for an anonymous check from God, we dismiss the two grocery coupon flyers as junk mail. A single woman may be desperately lonely and longing for a husband; she turns down an invitation to Ladies Day because it's a man she wants, not more women from church. A burnt-out businesswoman prays for a weeklong vacation on an island somewhere, but she overlooks the calm that a walk with her Golden Retriever can bring.

That's where our minds need renewal. God longs to fill you and transform you, and this exodus from oppression into freedom in Christ is a process, not a one-time fix. We don't get to give God a list of items we need from the Deliverance Market or treat the Holy Spirit as our personal assistant.

Submission to God means total surrender. This means we don't just lay down our chains and run to freedom in jogging shoes of our choice. We must also let go of our travel itinerary. God hears us, and He will answer us. But He does not restrict Himself to our plans, and—thank God for this—sometimes He doesn't even make sense.

The Nation of Israel: Key Concepts

Read Exodus 3 as you identify these key concepts.

1. Why did Moses "turn aside" to look at the burning bush? (Exodus 3:3; also Acts 7:31)

2. What happened when he turned to look? (Exodus 3:4)

3. After assuring Moses that He has seen the Israelites' agony and wants to deliver them, God then says what? (Exodus 3:10)

4. Describe Moses's reaction. (Exodus 3:11)

5. What qualifies Moses to do this work? (Exodus 3:12)

6. How was Moses supposed to introduce this plan to the people of Israel? (Exodus 3:14-15)

7. Why does God plan to send plagues on Egypt? (Exodus 3:19)

_____

_____

_____

_____

_____

_____

_____

_____

_____

Thinking it through . . .

1. What do you imagine Moses was thinking when God—seemingly nonchalantly—says that He's going to send Moses to Pharaoh so the Israelites can leave Egypt?

2. Consider the relationship between the Egyptians and the Israelites at this point (see the text from Exodus 1 if you need a reminder). How outlandish was God's plan?

3. What parts of this plan seem to make no sense at all?

_____

_____

_____

_____

_____

_____

_____

_____

_____

The Church: Key Concepts

1. Read Acts 13:38-41. What happens through Jesus Christ? (Verse 39)

2. What warning is given in this passage? (Verse 40)

3. To see what God was doing, one had to _____ (Verse 41); these works would not necessarily make sense. (Verse 41)

4. How are man's plans different than God's plans? (Acts 5:38-39; Isaiah 55:8-9)

_____

_____

_____

_____

_____

_____

_____

_____

Thinking it through . . .

1. What stories in the New Testament show us God working in ways that don't make sense so that His love and salvation can be shown to the lost?

2. Do you think today's Church misses God's hand sometimes because His work doesn't look like we expect it to look?

3. Is there a time in your life when God moved in a way that definitely wasn't what you would have chosen? How do you see His goodness in retrospect?

4. In thinking about sin, destructive patterns, or stagnancy that may be present in your life, what do you envision when you pray deliverance (relief, peace, freedom, etc.)?

5. What other ways might God choose to work His will in you?

_____

_____

_____

_____

_____

_____

_____

_____

God Leaves Nothing to Chance
(EXODUS 4-6)

LIFE LESSON 4
God expects your complete obedience.

Have you ever heard someone say, "God has a special plan for that child"? The well-meaning person is usually referring to a child who has an incredible talent or perhaps has overcome an enormous obstacle. But, truth be told, Scripture doesn't support God's picking favorites. In fact, God's track record is to appoint the available, not just the talented.

Who was more available than a passionate Israelite trying to keep a low profile among sheep? After some serious arguing with God, Moses musters up the nerve to ask his boss/father-in-law for some time off. I like how he downplays his reason for going— "to see whether [my brothers] are still alive." God must have sighed and shaken His head at Moses's pitch to Jethro, but He wastes no time in reminding Moses of what is about to happen.

This is crazy. I'm crazy. God is crazy, Moses must have been thinking. Looking at the staff in his hand that practically still hisses a reptilian reminder, Moses knows this is for real. All of his reasoning with God was useless: God has called him, and that is that.

Bless God eternally for His patience with all of Moses's doubts and certainly with all of ours. But make no mistake: God draws a line between self-doubt and disobedience. Calling or no calling, when Moses defied God, God hunted him down with a vengeance.

Moses was to lead God's people . . . incidentally, God's *circumcised* people . . . out of slavery, yet apparently he hadn't even circumcised his own son. My guess is that this disobedience wasn't a scream-in-your-face rebellion but, more likely, a casual omission—probably to avoid conflict with his wife Zipporah, who was not an Israelite, and thus probably not sold on inflicting this kind of pain on her precious baby boy.

The point appears to be, though, that Moses disobeyed. Disgruntled wife or not, Moses had a responsibility to uphold God's covenant, not to mention to lead by example. Ironically, it is Zipporah who grabs the scalpel when she realizes that God means business. She circumcises her own son, and God settles down.

God loves you to a ridiculous, nonsensical degree. But—hear this—He cannot and will not tolerate disobedience. You may have a conspicuous calling in the kingdom of God;

perhaps you even serve in full-time ministry or are respected for your Bible knowledge. But disobedience from you is just as putrid under God's nose as is disobedience from . . . well, *career* sinners, so to speak. I have no doubt that God would have raised up another leader if Moses did not finally obey. He will do the same with you if you willfully sustain a life of disobedience. You are replaceable. His holiness is not.

The Nation of Israel: Key Concepts

Read Exodus 4 as you identify these key concepts.

1. When Moses asks God how he will convince the Israelites that God indeed spoke to him, what is God's first question to him? (Exodus 4:2)

2. What else of Moses's does God use to build up a repertoire of signs? (Exodus 4:6)

3. Why does Moses qualify to be a speaker, despite his apparent speech impediment? (Exodus 4:12)

4. How does God feel about Moses's request that God find someone else? (Exodus 4:14)

5. When Moses and Aaron give God's message to the people, what is the nation's response? (Exodus 4:31)

_____

_____

_____

_____

_____

_____

_____

_____

Thinking it through . . .

1. What seems to be a theme in God's working through Moses?

2. What happens when God's people obey?

_____

_____

_____

_____

_____

_____

The Church: Key Concepts

1. When Jesus' eleven remaining disciples went to meet Jesus a final time, how did they respond when they saw Him? (Matthew 28:16-17)

2. What is Jesus' straightforward command for those who will build His Church? (Matthew 28:19)

3. Like God's response to Moses's doubt, what is Jesus' final promise? (Matthew 28:20)

_____

_____

_____

_____

_____

_____

_____

_____

Thinking it through . . .

1. God seems to be willing and desirous to use raw material. What may sometimes hold you back from complete obedience?

2. Is doubt a sin? How can doubt be enslaving?

3. What is our strongest qualification to do God's work—to obey the gospel?

_____

_____

_____

_____

_____

_____

_____

_____

_____

LIFE LESSON 5
Things might get worse before they get better.

There's nothing like waking up refreshed in the morning only to discover that Reality has already showered and made coffee. You opened your eyes encouraged—that God has your back, that today is the day that the Lord has made. But as soon as you peel back the covers and place your feet on the floor, Life takes over. In fact, Reality and Life got wind that you might dare to hope today, so they filled a U-Haul with bills, complaints, misbehaving kids, distant spouses, bitterness, and despair and headed straight for your driveway. What's worse—it appears God gave them directions to your house.

The Israelites were similarly gut-punched during their deliverance process. On the wings of worship, they were sure that God saw their suffering and planned to deliver them from slavery. Finally! Signs came through Aaron and Moses; the elders recognized God's hand, and the nation inhaled crisp, clean hope in the God of Abraham's desire to set them free from bondage. They bowed in worship. Perhaps they even danced and celebrated! After all, the God of Isaac and Abraham saw their suffering and promised to deliver them!

And then He went on vacation. Or so it must have seemed to the Israelites. I can imagine a spring in their steps and a fresh tune in their whistles as they rose to the daily rigor of brickmaking. Today, the sun's blistering rage wouldn't be as bothersome. Endless thirst could take a number because Yahweh was about to set them free.

Imagine their formidable despair, then, when their difficult task went from backbreaking to completely impossible. Before, they made bricks out of straw that was provided for them. Now, they were to go out and find their own straw each day and still manage to produce as many bricks as they had before.

I admit that this is precisely the type of story I prefer to skip when introducing a non-believer to God. This chapter is horrible PR for God, yet its solid place in the story of God's deliverance of His people prompts me to search for God's presence even in this mess.

Was God just being—. Go ahead. Ask. We've all wondered. *Was God just being cruel?*

You've probably wondered the same thing after being surprised by the co-existence of suffering and deliverance. Is God being cruel? Hasn't He promised to set us free? If that's true, then why are things only getting worse?

Your questions are precisely evocative of the Israelites' panic attack. If the exodus story ended here, we could perhaps make a fair assumption about God's so-called joke. But God . . . well, that's actually in the next lesson. For today, though, take comfort in those two words: *But God.* They are all the difference in the world between us and those who have no hope.

The Nation of Israel: Key Concepts
Read Exodus 5 as you identify these key concepts.

1. What did Moses and Aaron, on behalf of the Israelites, ask permission to do? (Exodus 5:1)

2. What did the pharaoh's anger lead him to do? (Exodus 5:6-8)

3. Of what did the pharaoh accuse the Israelites? (Exodus 5:17)

4. What is the Israelites' response to Moses and Aaron? (Exodus 5:21)

5. What is Moses's response to God? (Exodus 5:22-23)

_____

_____

_____

_____

_____

_____

_____

_____

_____

Thinking it through . . .

1. What do you think the pharaoh was most afraid of or bothered by?

2. Why do you think the Israelites' confidence in God was zapped so quickly?

3. Why do you think God allowed the Israelites to be tortured even more?

4. After the miraculous signs he had seen from God, Moses still challenges God. Does this surprise you? Have you ever struggled with faith even after seeing God's hand at work?

_____

_____

_____

_____

_____

_____

_____

_____

The Church: Key Concepts

1. What happened to the apostles as they started spreading the gospel? (Acts 5:17-18)

2. What was the reason for the high priest's (and the Sadducees) persecution of them? (Acts 5:17)

3. Read Acts 6:8-14. What was the Freedmen's accusation against Stephen?

4. What happened to Stephen after he testified? (Acts 7:58)

_____

_____

_____

_____

_____

_____

_____

_____

_____

Thinking it through . . .

1. Do you struggle to understand and appreciate suffering? Does it make you angry at God or shaky in your faith?

2. When you are trying to obey God and trying to live a godly life, do you ever see your suffering just continue? Does this discourage you in your faith?

3. In what ways are you still struggling—perhaps after much prayer and effort, nothing seems to be changing?

_____

_____

_____

LIFE LESSON 5: *Things might get worse before they get better.*

_____

_____

_____

_____

_____

_____

LIFE LESSON 6
God is the LORD. Enough said.

It seems the most commonly asked question of God is *why. Why, God? Why did my marriage have to end in divorce? Why didn't you heal my child of cancer? Why didn't you provide money for us to pay our rent? Why, Lord? Why?*

To our dismay, of course, God seems to rarely answer that question—at least not at the moment we ask it. As a parent of two strong, adventurous, independent boys, I find myself often not answering the "why" questions either. Sometimes it's because I don't want to nurture an argument and listen to one of them rebut every reason I give as to *why* he can't climb on the roof to get the debris from his rocket. Sometimes, though, it's simply because I want to assert my authority in a situation where I suspect it's being questioned.

"Because I said so" actually strikes me as a scriptural response from a parent to a child when said with the loving aim of teaching submission to authority. How do I know this? Check out Exodus 6:1.

With Moses prostrate in grief, frustration, and angst—begging God for a sneak peak of His purpose—God simply continues the conversation from a couple chapters back. There's no coddling of Moses. No reassurance that Moses was doing a good job. No wiping of his tears. In the face of Moses's doubting cries, God seemingly skips over the "why" and says this: "I am the Lord" (Exodus 6:2).

He then proceeds to remind Moses of His identity and His promise to the Israelites, ending with the same definitive statement: "I am the Lord" (Exodus 6:8). So I'm thinking this *is* God's answer to "why." I'm not sure poor Moses caught on, though, and I can't say I blame him.

He tried again with the Israelites, and, naturally, they weren't so excited this time around since the last pep rally with Moses led to further abuse from the Egyptians. Moses returns to God—Who, incidentally, is now ready for Moses to approach Pharaoh himself, for heaven's sake—and complains again of his limitations. "I am of uncircumcised lips," he reminds God again in verses 12 and 30. A common Hebrew figure of speech for a physical flaw, Moses was essentially saying, "God, I have a speech impediment" and . . . in case He didn't hear . . . "God, I have a speech impediment."

But God. That's it. That's the essence of today's lesson. The reason we can do anything He commands us to do—the reason we can surrender any bad habit, feel complete without our modern-day idols, or divest ourselves of sin—is that *He is*. He is LORD. As in, bigger than anything. As in, ruler of all.

But I sound like Foghorn Leghorn when I talk, Moses argued. But God. *But I've tried a million times to change, and I just can't,* you think. But God. He is LORD, and that might just be the answer to all of our "whys." He is LORD.

Enough said.

The Nation of Israel: Key Concepts

Read Exodus 6 as you identify these key concepts.

1. How does God say that the pharaoh will send the Israelites away? (Exodus 6:1)
2. What is one qualification God gives of His own identity? (Exodus 6:3-5)
3. What is one promise God makes for the Israelites? (Exodus 6:6-8)
4. Why didn't the people of Israel listen to Moses this time? (Exodus 6:9)
5. Read Moses's complaint in Exodus 6:12, 30. Does God seem to address this at all?

_____

_____

_____

_____

_____

_____

_____

_____

Thinking it through . . .

1. Why do you think God answers Moses with an immediate reminder of how ugly Pharaoh was going to get—it's like God was saying with boyish excitement, "Just wait 'til you see what I'm gonna do to him!" How does this seem like a decent response to Moses's groanings?
2. Which part of God's message for the Israelites do you think they probably challenged the most?
3. Think about Moses's speech issue. What might be the Israelites' reaction to hearing him speak? How might the pharaoh react to hearing Moses actually talk?

_____

_____

_____

_____

_____

_____

_____

_____

_____

The Church: Key Concepts

1. Where does God's Spirit dwell now? (1 Corinthians 3:16)

2. What is God calling us to leave behind? (Colossians 3:5 and 8)

3. What is the prize—the promise land, so to speak—for today's Christians? (1 Timothy 6:12)

_____

_____

_____

_____

_____

_____

_____

_____

_____

Thinking it through . . .

1. What are some of your own limitations, weaknesses, or fears?

2. Do you feel close-minded to certain forms of ministry because of these? (For example, maybe you're a bad cook, so you don't even nod in the direction of a family who needs a meal.)

3. Are we as self-conscious about the sin in our lives as we are about our earthly limitations? Why or why not?

_____

_____

_____

_____

_____

_____

_____

_____

✴ SESSION 3 ✴

God Won't Leave You for Dead
(EXODUS 7-9)

LIFE LESSON 7
Deliverance begins with water and blood.

M aybe I'm reaching here, but I can't get over the apparent significance of the nature of the first plague: Water is turned into blood. The miraculous deliverance of God's people from years of slavery begins with the transformation of *water* into *blood*.

Could God be asserting His long-term plan for our salvation along a riverbed full of hemoglobin? Centuries later, we are delivered from our kinship to the powers of darkness by the blood of Jesus Christ. As we confess Jesus as Lord and the waters of baptism cover us completely, the blood of Jesus washes our sins away. Fortunately, however, we are spared the frogs and boils and other pestilences that the Egyptians had to exchange as legal tender for their tight grip on God's beloved people.

But our cost was just as great—actually, much more pricey than a bulk order of fly swatters or some shovels to clear away the hail. Like a true Gentleman in love with His future bride, the sovereign King of the universe picked up our tab. If only a credit card could cover this one! You know, however, what the Payment had to be: God's own Son.

I received a humbling glimpse into the size of God's invoice several years ago. My body had never quite recovered from three pregnancies, and months after my youngest son was born, a serious illness put me in the hospital in need of an immediate blood transfusion. Even as the IV lines were being strung, I tried to delay the process, asking for time for a family member to fly in so that I could at least receive blood from someone I knew. No. I had to have blood right then.

Pint by pint, thousands of dollars later, the blood needed to save my life left in its wake a medical bill that left me speechless. Though insurance would write the check, I still could not get over *how expensive blood was*. I had tried to get it my own way—from a family member—but my need was bigger than my plan. Despite the tremendous cost, the only answer was to accept the life-saving drip that had been special ordered for my type and delivered in a cooler by a courier working overtime.

Oh, how typical this is of our vain attempts to fund our own forgiveness. What we need is the costly, lifesaving blood of Jesus, but instead we try to cover our shame with a new pair of shoes. Or another daytime soap opera. We try to soothe our loneliness on Facebook or placate our worries by sharing prayer requests that we never actually lift to God ourselves. In the same way that your preschooler's plastic coins and toy dollars would look foolish as tender for your groceries, our at-home-remedies for sin are equally value-less.

Maybe you haven't actually begun your transformation. Maybe you've been billing alcohol or illicit relationships for the cost of your sin instead of God. If this is you, stop. Accept God's salvation! Let Him pay your debt! Confess your need for a Savior. Confess that Jesus is Lord, and be baptized into Him for the forgiveness of your sins (Acts 2:38)* The waters of baptism activate the blood of Jesus Christ—you become a child of God!

And you are set free.

* *For more references to the role of baptism in your salvation, see the following verses: Matthew 28:19; Mark 16:16; John 3:5; Acts 2:41; Acts 22:16; Romans 6:3-4; 1 Corinthians 12:13; Galatians 3:27; Ephesians 5:26; Colossians 2:12; 1 Peter 3:21.*

The Nation of Israel: Key Concepts
Read Exodus 7 as you identify these key concepts.

1. What two things will God be doing in preparation for this exodus? (Exodus 7:3)
2. What two things are the sorcerers able to do right along with Moses and Aaron? (Exodus 7:10-11 and 21-22)
3. Does God have Moses and Aaron simply sneak out to the Nile to turn it into blood? (Verses 15 and 20)

_____

_____

_____

_____

_____

_____

_____

_____

_____

Thinking it through . . .

1. What do you think Moses's thoughts were toward God after experiencing perhaps some slight relief (Aaron would actually be the one to talk to the pharaoh) and immediate discouragement (Pharaoh isn't going to go for this)? (Exodus 7:2-4)

2. Verse 19 indicates that all water would be turned to blood, not just the river. If this were to happen in our modern-day homes, what would that look like?

3. Let's not miss an important point of reflection: Exodus 7:20a. What seems key to deliverance?

_____

_____

_____

_____

_____

_____

_____

_____

_____

The Church: Key Concepts

1. Read 1 Corinthians 10:2. What term does Paul use for the process of the Hebrews' becoming followers of Moses?

2. Read Hebrews 9:22. What is absolutely required for the forgiveness of sins?

3. Read 1 Peter 3:20-21. What did God do for Noah and his family? How does this relate to us?

_____

_____

_____

_____

_____

_____

_____

_____

_____

Thinking it through . . .

1. What are ways we try to earn forgiveness and/or numb the awareness of our sin?

2. It seems clear that our exodus from the slavery of sin begins with water. How would you explain this to a believer who does not believe baptism is a scriptural requirement?

3. Have you received Christ's forgiveness through Jesus' shed blood on the cross? Have you been cleansed in the waters of baptism? If not, are you ready to do so?

_____

_____

_____

_____

_____

_____

_____

_____

LIFE LESSON 8
Deliverance stinks.

If the Israelites had any sweet dreams of being whisked away as if in a fairy tale, they were certainly living reality TV now. Blood everywhere was nasty, but secretly maybe they enjoyed watching the Egyptians scrounge for hydration. Dead frogs in heaps, however . . . well, that just *stank* (Exodus 8:14).

Because I've been unfortunate enough to smell a dead rodent or two, I can imagine this was absolutely wretched. Though the plagues were against the Egyptians, the Israelites certainly had to keep working with these people. In their land. With their frogs. With their *dead* frogs.

Though we can look at the entire book of Exodus and see these plagues as part of God's miraculous plan of deliverance, the Israelites didn't have that advantage. I'm guessing that the smell of death likely wasn't potpourri to them, despite their promised freedom. Gnats and flies everywhere, too! I can think of many worldly phrases right now that probably captured some of their thoughts as they continued their backbreaking labor day after day without so much as a can of bug spray.

Does this sound like sweet release to you? Are you nodding your head as you read this chapter, with a *been there, done that* sensation sweeping over you? You're praying daily for your husband's temper to be calmed by the Holy Spirit, but after one counseling session, his next explosion is worse than ever. You would gladly spend quiet time each day with God, but your small children are sucking the life out of you. You know you are seeking the right thing, but something is just rotten.

Of the human body's five senses, brain science says that our sense of smell is the sense most linked to memory. Unlike sights, sounds, and other senses, smells do not make any pit stops on their way to the brain. They are processed immediately and can trigger memories even years later. To this day I abhor the scent of vanilla. Why? Almost fifteen years ago, a vanilla air freshener in my kitchen triggered morning sickness during my first pregnancy.

I'm not entirely sure what God's logic was in selecting frogs, gnats, and flies. I mean, why not chickens, mosquitos, and lizards? Or any other animal reproduced *ad nauseam*, for that matter? But I'm thinking that when these suckers started dying off—oh, gag me—the stench of death in the noses of the Israelites would perhaps serve as a powerful memory for them some day. Perhaps it was necessary evidence of the process of death.

Romans 6 reminds us that our *life* with Christ means our *death* to sin. And dying stinks, remember? The stench of death is evidence of the death itself. So, actually, I'm feeling a *hallelujah* here! *Something has died!* And if that something is sin, you are doing everything right.

The Nation of Israel: Key Concepts
Read Exodus 8 as you identify these key concepts.

1. Were the magicians able to reproduce the plague of the frogs? (Exodus 8:7) Is there any evidence that they were able to get rid of it?

2. Were the magicians able to reproduce the plague of the gnats? (Exodus 8:18)

3. How does your Bible read for Exodus 8:23? (State which translation you have.)

4. Why did Moses not compromise on where his people offered sacrifices to God? (Exodus 8:26)

_____

_____

_____

_____

_____

_____

_____

_____

_____

Thinking it through . . .

1. Close your eyes and get a mental picture of Exodus 8:3,4. If necessary, picture this plague in your own house.

2. Why do you think God didn't just scoop the frogs up when Exodus 8:11 was promised? Why did the dead ones have to be piled up so that the odor permeated the land?

3. What are your thoughts as to why the magicians no longer had power to replicate the plagues after the frogs?

_____

_____

_____

_____

_____

_____

_____

_____

_____

The Church: Key Concepts

1. Read James 1:12. After considering the stench of death, what is one more reason we have to rejoice when "life stinks"?

2. Read Galatians 6:9. Why shouldn't we give up in doing the right thing?

3. Read Romans 6:5. What is our wonderful hope amidst death?

_____

_____

_____

_____

_____

_____

_____

_____

_____

Thinking it through . . .

1. Let's think of an alcoholic trying to get sober. In what ways would death to alcohol and addiction "stink"?

2. When have you smelled the stench of death in your walk with Christ? What was this like for you?

3. Read Exodus 8:25-27 again. Do you think it's possible to worship God while living in bondage to sin?

_____

_____

_____

_____

_____

_____

_____

_____

LIFE LESSON 9
Warning comes before destruction.

I'm not sure that paying attention to warnings is a natural instinct for humans. Most kids don't hold good track records for heeding their parents' protective warnings to "not touch" or "stay away from that," but before you roll your eyes at kids these days, let's admit together that we adults aren't a whole lot better at appreciating destruction's heads-up.

Financial expert Dave Ramsey vehemently warns listeners against the dangers of credit card debt, yet I've heard many respond with, "He's talking about people who go overboard. We use them responsibly." As I write, nutritionists are plastering warning signs everywhere about processed foods and toxins like high fructose corn syrup or partially hydrogenated anything—but excuse me while I take another sip of my soda.

I'm not trying to pronounce judgment on people who use credit cards or, heaven help me and my pantry, consume processed foods. My concern is for more significant warnings that we are, unfortunately, no less prone to simply ignore: warnings about sin.

I don't want to spend eternity in hell, and I'm guessing that's not on your post-mortem wish list either. *But why do I keep sinning?* Because I'm ignoring the warnings. Though painful to admit, I know that disrespect of my husband is a sin, yet when I want my way, I toss out the warning in Ephesians 5. I know that deception is a sin, yet when I want to use an expired coupon, I bury Colossians 3:9 right in the middle of the stack where I hope the cashier won't notice or care about the invalid savings.

In the same way my protective husband, who loves me as Christ loves the Church, warns me about an icy spot on a sidewalk or a shallow dip that might cause me to stumble in a parking lot, God warns us about disaster on the horizon. Exodus 9 shows God's warning Pharaoh intentionally about what was coming next if he continued to exalt himself above the God of the Israelites.

In fact, God's heart seems physically pained as He says to Pharaoh through Moses, "For if you refuse . . . the hand of the Lord will fall with a very severe plague" (verses 2-3). Given that God wants absolutely none of us to go to hell—to "perish" (2 Peter 3:9)—I'm thinking that His heart is equally pained when He warns us of our own sin.

"For the wages of sin is death" (Romans 6:23), and not just big-time sins like murder or adultery. *Sin* encompasses all our turnings from God, and the penalty is death regardless of how many people were hurt or who found out. Jesus paid that penalty, but Romans 1:18-32 reminds us that God will have no mercy on those of us who, having received the truth of the gospel, still choose sin as our dance partner.

Today let's make a point to reflect on our covert sins. The easy-to-hide, easy-to-explain, so-smooth-you-even-see-them-in-church sins. With the same vigor and urgency with which we would attack a roach in our kitchen, let's wage war on these pesky "little" sins in our lives. If we don't, we are in danger of losing our souls.

Be warned. And do the only right thing: *repent.*

The Nation of Israel: Key Concepts

Read Exodus 9 as you identify these key concepts.

1. God gives his specific warning in Exodus 9:2-3, but He takes an additional step in Exodus 9:5. What is that?

2. What will be unique about the plague of hail? (Exodus 9:14)

3. What protection did God extend over His people? (Exodus 9:6, 26)

4. What is the fundamental reason that God keeps sending plagues on Egypt? (Exodus 9:17)

_____

_____

_____

_____

_____

_____

_____

_____

Thinking it through . . .

1. All the plagues were awful, but why do you think the plague on the livestock was "very severe"?

2. What do you make of God being the One responsible for hardening Pharaoh's heart?

3. How has God actually shown restraint with the Egyptians up to this point?

_____

_____

_____

_____

_____

_____

_____

_____

_____

The Church: Key Concepts

1. What is God's warning to us about sin? (Romans 6:23)

2. Do any of us know when we will face Judgment? (Matthew 24:36)

3. Will God protect and preserve the Church amidst destruction in the world? (John 16:33) Under what condition? (John 14:15)

_____

_____

_____

_____

_____

_____

_____

_____

Thinking it through . . .

1. At what point in our spiritual journey do you think we are most conscientious about sin? How can we stay in a state of vigilance about our hearts?

2. Do you think the church in Laodicea that Scripture describes as "lukewarm" (Revelation 3:15-16) had perhaps lost their conscientiousness about sin?

_____

_____

_____

_____

_____

_____

_____

_____

✦ SESSION 4 ✦

God Always Leaves an Impression
(EXODUS 10-12)

LIFE LESSON 10

There is no darkness like darkness without God.

A few years ago, I took my sons on a day trip to Mammoth Cave. Our tour through the massive underground space was dimly lit, and, like any mom, I spent the entire time reaching for my kids to make sure we stayed together in this dark basement of Kentucky. I soon realized, however, that this barely visible room was a Vegas strip compared to the natural lighting capacity of a cave.

With only a brief warning, our guide turned off the footlights, allowing us to experience the cave in its raw state. That's when I felt it. I *felt* darkness. There was no adjusting my eyes to a tolerable night vision. There were no cracks or pockets of light to offer relief. As thick as my mother's beef stew, darkness settled ominously on my nose, eclipsing all of my reflexes.

They don't even make crayons that dark. My "blackest black" mascara is, in fact, pastel now that I know what the *blackest black* really is.

I wanted to reach for my kids, but I felt paralyzed. Terrified to move even an inch, my only assurance was that their soft voices of awe arose right beside me. My knees locked. My neck stiffened. Whereas seconds earlier I was the strong, protective mommy blazing a safe path for my kids, I was now powerless and completely vulnerable.

This must be what darkness feels like without God. Like a steaming, sticky vat of freshly mixed asphalt, life without God is an inescapable blackness that clings to every aspect of our lives.

As if metric tons of grasshoppers weren't enough, Pharaoh has again hardened his heart and refused to let God's people leave. This time—and don't miss the timing of this plague right before God's *coup de grace*—God has sent darkness. Not just the Alaskan, nighttime-six-months-at-a-time kind of darkness. God has commanded Moses to sequester "a darkness to be felt" (Exodus 10:21).

Like me in the cave, the Egyptians are completely immobilized. Nobody moves for three days. Nobody, that is, except the Israelites, who are still able to plug in their lamps and feel the warmth of the sun. God's favor was upon them; therefore, they had Light.

There is darkness. Like our front door at night when we're fumbling for our house key and the porch light has blown out. Or the first few seconds of an indoor thrill ride at an amusement park where all the creepy crawlies are getting in position.

But then there is *darkness to be felt*. The blackest black. Suffocating, paralyzing, impenetrable nothingness. The Egyptians lived this for three terrifying days, and Scripture suggests that a few of them were getting the message: God wasn't playing around.

Our exodus begins with obedience and a willingness to repent from whatever sin entangles us and turn our hearts toward God. Not even military night vision technology can help us if we don't.

The Nation of Israel: Key Concepts
Read Exodus 10 as you identify these key concepts.

1. What would be especially devastating about the plague of locusts? (Exodus 10:5, referring back to Exodus 9:31-32)
2. What are two compromises Pharaoh offered Moses? (Exodus 10:10-11 and 24)
3. What was the plague of darkness like for the Egyptians? (Exodus 10:23)

_____

_____

_____

_____

_____

_____

_____

_____

Thinking it through . . .

1. Perhaps a plague of locusts seems like a step down in severity. But how did the combination of the locusts and the darkness simulate life without God?
2. Moses wouldn't budge an inch on the conditions for the Hebrew exodus. What do you think would have happened if he had agreed, for example, to leave behind the children or the livestock?

3. Extreme darkness has some side effects. What are these?

_____

_____

_____

_____

_____

_____

_____

The Church: Key Concepts

1. Read Psalm 139:11. What does this teach us about God's relationship to darkness?

2. Read Matthew 27:45. What happened in the middle of the day as Jesus was hanging on the cross? How widespread was this?

3. Read Matthew 8:12. What will take place in the "outer darkness"?

_____

_____

_____

_____

_____

_____

_____

Thinking it through . . .

1. Can God find you in the thickest darkness? How do you know?

2. Have you ever been through a dark season in life? Was it *dark* or *darkness to be felt*? What were some of the side effects of that darkness?

3. Think of the role of fear in darkness. Is it possible to be in the dark and not be afraid?

_____

_____

_____

_____

_____

_____

_____

_____

LIFE LESSON 11

God distinguishes between the sacred and the secular.

Sometimes we are in bondage because we have sinned. A lot. Probably even on purpose. A few "innocent" winks to a guy in your night class has turned into long conversations on break and texts in the late hours of the evenings. Before you know it, you have selected adultery from sin's scrumptious buffet line. Predictably, it tasted good going down, but it has poisoned your soul and ruined those you love. You are in bondage, and it is your fault.

Other times we feel crushed beneath circumstances completely outside our ability to control. Tragedy hits like a wrecking ball, and you have no chance to catch your breath. Your teenage daughter has attempted suicide for the third time. Your heart breaks as you check her into a rehabilitation clinic, only to discover that your insurance has denied coverage for this expensive, but necessary treatment. Meanwhile, your elderly parents have left you three voicemails asking you to help them put up their Christmas decorations. You feel completely leveled by the ruthlessness of life, and it isn't your fault at all.

As his eyes readjusted to seeing light again, Pharaoh was in trouble, and it was indeed his fault. He had hardened his heart toward God, and even the local pest control businesses no longer wanted to take his calls. In fact, many of his own servants and civilians were crossing their fingers that Pharaoh would hang up his ego and honor the Hebrew God.

The Israelites, of course, were still in slavery, and it was not their fault. They were willing to leave Egypt to follow Moses to the land promised to Abraham, Isaac, and Jacob. They were willing to go sacrifice to Yahweh, the great I Am. But their chains were forged, and they could do nothing but wait for deliverance.

As testimony to His steadfast love, God had a message for both Pharaoh and the Israelites. As opposed to spontaneously wiping out hardhearted Pharaoh and capsizing his entire kingdom under his Egyptian toes, God sends him one final warning—a message about what was to come as a result of his sin, his turning from God. For the Israelites, God's message is simple: Get ready. Start gathering up your stuff, and pick up your going-away gifts from your neighbors.

God loves you like crazy, but He is not ambivalent about the nature of your oppression. In the same way He distinguished between the Egyptians and the Israelites, He draws a line between the sacred and the secular. If you are living in sin but going around feeling sorry for yourself, God's message to you is a warning: Turn from your sin, and He will set you free with forgiveness (1 John 1:8-9). If you are being beaten down by the pressures of life, God has a message for you, too: Press on (2 Corinthians 4:8-10; 1 Corinthians 4:2).

Look in the mirror, and be honest about your chains.

The Nation of Israel: Key Concepts

Read Exodus 11 as you identify these key concepts.

1. How does God say that Pharaoh will drive the Israelites away? (Exodus 11:1)

2. How did the Egyptians feel about Moses and the Israelites by now? (Exodus 11:3)

3. What time will God come with the next plague? (Exodus 11:4)

4. What will this plague be? (Exodus 11:5)

5. How will God distinguish between the sinful and the holy? (Exodus 11:7)

_____

_____

_____

_____

_____

_____

_____

_____

_____

Thinking it through . . .

1. Why is it significant that Pharaoh will drive the Israelites out "completely"?

2. Why do you think God chose to send the angel of death at midnight?

3. Why did God protect the Israelites?

_____

_____

_____

_____

_____

_____

_____

_____

The Church: Key Concepts

1. Read Revelation 2:9-11. Why was the church in Smyrna experiencing oppression?
   What is John's message (God's promise) to them in verse 11?

2. Read Revelation 3:1-3. Why was the church in Sardis in bondage?
   What is John's message (God's promise) to them in verse 3?

_____

_____

_____

_____

_____

_____

_____

_____

_____

Thinking it through . . .

1. What kinds of thoughts do you think were going through the minds of those in the
   church in Smyrna? In Sardis?

2. What is ironic about the difference between your two answers?
   What can we learn from this?

_____

_____

_____

_____

_____

_____

_____

_____

_____

LIFE LESSON 12
Remember the Lord's goodness. Always.

A dear friend of mine nearly lost her youngest child in a massive car accident several years ago. Completely unrecognizable due to broken bones and massive blood loss, little Kimmy was in a critical care unit for weeks. Despite numerous reconstructive surgeries on the horizon for the next decade as Kimmy's body continued to grow, my sweet friend danced with joy that her daughter's life was saved and that what could have been every parent's worst nightmare actually turned into a miraculous recovery.

Though years have passed, my friend remembers that day well. In fact, she rides an emotional tilt-o-whirl each year on the anniversary date of the car wreck. On the one hand, she recalls with horror the initially gory, monstrous appearance of her beautiful, petite, long-haired girl and the simultaneous tsunami of fear she felt when Kimmy's condition was not yet stabilized. On the other hand, however, she cries crocodile mommy tears and offers thanksgiving to God for sparing her daughter's life and restoring her overall health.

Either way, she remembers.

Nobody will ever know Kimmy or her mom without hearing this story.

Do we remember God's work in our lives with the same tenacity? Do I celebrate the anniversary of my baptism into Christ with the same excitement with which I anticipate gifts on my natural birthday? Do my kids even know the story of how I came to Christ? What about the time I was carrying a heavy weight of grief after a family tragedy? Do I regularly honor God by sharing with others how He loved me through that awful season?

In Exodus 12, God was about to take over a half-million Israelites on a one-way trip to freedom, but before He let them board the bus, He established one rule: Remember. Through the Feast of Unleavened Bread—remember. Through the Passover Feast—remember. Through the very way you even eat on the trip home—remember.

So much of your strength for the journey out of bondage will come from remembering how God has worked on your behalf in the past. Your children's spiritual heritage will be built on memories of their parents' journeys with God. More significant than even the family photo album or the box of love notes you and your husband have exchanged over the years will be the testimonies—even time-honored celebrations—of your victories in Christ.

You may be gasping for air under a yoke of anxiety and stress right now. God wants to lift it, so if you do anything as preparation, get out your camera or your journal.

This is going to be good!

The Nation of Israel: Key Concepts

Read Exodus 12 as you identify the following concepts.

1. What did God do to the Hebrew calendar with the Passover event? (Exodus 12:2)

2. What would God look for so that He could spare the Hebrew households from the punishment of death? (Exodus 12:13)

3. How long are the Israelites supposed to remember and honor this miraculous event? (Exodus 12:14, 17, 24)

4. What are God's instructions for how to answer children's questions about this annual memorial? (Exodus 12:26, 27)

5. Why were the Israelites able to leave Egypt with so much bounty? (Exodus 12:35-36)

6. Why did they have to eat unleavened bread? (Exodus 12:39)

7. What time of day was it when the Israelites left? What was God doing during this time? (Exodus 12:42)

_____

_____

_____

_____

_____

_____

_____

_____

_____

Thinking it through . . .

1. The nation of Israel was centuries old by now, but how did the exodus mark a beginning for them?

2. Why do you think God wanted them to be so intentional about remembering the Passover?

3. Do you find it significant that God led them out during darkness?

_____

_____

_____

_____

_____

_____

_____

_____

_____

_____

The Church: Key Concepts

1. What does God look for in His pardoning of us? (Hebrews 9:22)

2. How are Christians supposed to remember Christ's ultimate act of deliverance? (Luke 22:19; 1 Corinthians 11:24) To what main item of physical sustenance did Jesus equate Himself? (John 6:35)

3. What happened to the sky when Jesus died on the cross? (Luke 23:44-45)

_____

_____

_____

_____

_____

_____

_____

_____

Thinking it through . . .

1. Other than holidays, sacraments, or celebrations, what are other ways you can remember God's work in your life?

2. What does it mean to you that Jesus is "the Bread of life"?

3. The Israelites were led out of Egypt in darkness. Darkness covered the earth when our exodus began. What are you learning about darkness?

_____

_____

_____

_____

_____

_____

_____

_____

God Will Never Leave You Behind

(EXODUS 13-17)

LIFE LESSON 13

God may lead you out the long way.

I have absolutely zero sense of direction. In fact, I am never more insecure than when I am driving in an unfamiliar area. The invention of the GPS made my life infinitesimally easier, especially since I'm not even blessed with the drive-it-once-never-forget-it instinct. Even more embarrassing, I have trouble finding my way home from unfamiliar places, and Lord help me if I get detoured for any reason!

My favorite feature of the first GPS I ever owned was the "Home" icon. I had stored my home address in the device; so no matter where I was, I could always hit "Home," and immediately the path to my house would be narrated by that familiar, robotic voice.

Occasionally, I've noticed that my GPS will direct me on a route that seems to make no sense. *What the heck?* I'll complain, as if I could reason with technology—or, frankly, as if I had even half the sense of direction God gave a walrus. Nonetheless, I still get irritated when the route is longer or more time-consuming than I think it should be.

I imagine the Israelites were feeling the same irritation when, after finally being sanctioned to leave by Pharaoh, they hung a sharp right instead of moving straight ahead. *For the love of Pete, why can't God do anything simply?* they must have been thinking. Moses was probably trembling in fear of a revolt. Logic said to march straight out of Egypt through the land of the Philistines; God, not surprisingly, led them out the long way.

As we're about to learn, God had indeed hit the "Home" button on the Israelites' GPS. Though the route seemed insensible, God had His reasons, and those reasons were completely focused on taking them to their promised land.

You've probably noticed that healing, repentance, and recovery are rarely easy. *Why couldn't God just help me to quit smoking cold turkey? Why can't I win the lottery to pay off all these debts? Why do I still have to work with the man I used to fantasize about?* I don't have the answer to all of those questions, but let's remember God's apparent answer to all of our "why" questions (from Exodus 6): He is the Lord. Enough said. We are to honor His authority and obey Him unconditionally.

So as you leave the yoke of oppression and begin your first lap around the track to freedom in Christ, rest assured that God is the voice in your spiritual GPS. He may take you the long way, but He knows the way home.

After all, He *is* the map.

The Nation of Israel: Key Concepts

Read Exodus 13 as you identify these key concepts.

1. How did the Lord bring the Israelites out of Egypt? (Exodus 13:3, 9)
2. Why did God lead the Israelites the long way around as they left Egypt? (Exodus 13:17)
3. What type of environment did God lead them through? (Exodus 13:18)
4. Describe the Israelites' level of readiness to wage battle at this point. (Exodus 13:18)
5. Whose bones did Moses bring with them? (Exodus 13:19)
6. How did God lead the Israelites during the day? (Exodus 13:21)
7. How did He lead them at night? (Exodus 13:21)
8. Did these signs ever leave them while they were on their journey? (Exodus 13:22)

Thinking it through . . .

1. Do you think that God sometimes spares us "the easy way out" because it would, in fact, cause us to run back into bondage?
2. Why do you think the Israelites were able to be "battle-ready" at this point?
3. How could the cloud by day and the fire by night be seen as a nuisance? How could they be seen as a blessing?

_____

_____

_____

_____

_____

_____

_____

_____

_____

The Church: Key Concepts

1. Read John 14:6. What does Jesus call Himself in this passage?

2. Read Acts 24:14. What was the sect of Christ-followers called in the early Church?

3. Read Acts 1:9. How was Jesus taken off the physical earth?

4. Read Luke 21:27. How will Jesus return to the physical earth?

5. Read Matthew 3:11. How did John say that Jesus would baptize?

6. Read Acts 2:3. How did the Holy Spirit manifest Himself with the apostles?

_____

_____

_____

_____

_____

_____

_____

_____

Thinking it through . . .

1. Why do you think it is so hard for us to enjoy "the journey" and be less concerned with how things all end up?

2. What is uncomfortable about fire?

3. What do you dislike about clouds?

4. Can you think of a time when God led you out of a rough spot "the long way," so to speak? What did that look like?

_____

_____

_____

_____

_____

_____

_____

_____

LIFE LESSON 14
God fights for you.

When I was about 10, my sister and I often met up with other neighborhood kids to "ride the ditch" with our bikes. "The ditch" was a steep dip in a mound of dirt on a vacant lot down the street. Always the smallest child, I typically remained a spectator as my big sister challenged the boys down the ditch. The trick was not only to make it down the ditch without falling off their bikes, but also to make it back up the other side without succumbing to gravity before once again reaching the plateau.

One day I actually worked up the nerve to try the ditch. I backed up for a speedy start so that I would have enough momentum to make it up the opposite side without falling. My sister—always my best friend and protector—was on the other side cheering for me, and a few neighborhood kids looked on indifferently. Swallowing my fear, I dipped down the ditch, letting the wind blow my pigtails like windsocks behind me.

I made it down with impressive agility. Making it back up the other side, however, was a different story. My little legs spinning, I couldn't control the massive flop my bike took, nor could I manage to climb out from under it before the next ditch rider swooned down.

He flew down as if on wings, ran over me like I was just an annoying speed bump, and effortlessly made it back up the other side. Naturally, I started crying, though I think it was more out of embarrassment than for being injured in any way.

By the time I managed to walk my bike back up the ditch, the knight rider who had just lit over me was cowering under my sister's angry words. She leaned over him and threatened to knock his block off. He dared to retaliate, and she raised her fist at him. Before I knew it, she was chasing a terrified boy down the street, where he managed to barely make it in his front door without her leveling him flat.

I think of this scene often when I think of God as our mighty Warrior. And, sure enough, Exodus 14 shows God hot on the tail of the Egyptians who were out to reclaim their Hebrew slaves. With even more vengeance than my sister's barreling down the street like a racehorse, God relentlessly pursues the Egyptians, burying them with muddy waters before they even had a chance to cower away.

God fights for *you* with that same fervor. His passion is for your soul, and He does not sit idle while Satan does cartwheels over your heart. In the same way that you would rip to shreds anyone who tried to hurt one of your children, God exacts revenge when one of His beloved ones is being pursued.

If you fast forward about 64 books, you know that God wins. Your responsibility is to not step out of the ring before the clock runs out.

The Nation of Israel: Key Concepts

Read Exodus 14 as you identify these key concepts.

1. With the Passover barely behind them, what is Pharaoh's reaction to the exodus of the Israelites? (Exodus 14:5-7)

2. What is the reaction of the Israelites? (Exodus 14:10-11)

3. What was Moses's promise to them? (Exodus 14:14)

4. How did God tweak these directions just a little? (Exodus 14:15)

5. What happens to the cloud that had been leading the Israelites during the day? (Exodus 14:19)

6. Contrast the Israelites' crossing with the Egyptians' crossing of the Red Sea.

7. What did the Egyptians realize? (Exodus 14:25)

8. What evidence of victory did God allow the Israelites to see after the crossing? (Exodus 14:30)

_____

_____

_____

_____

_____

_____

_____

_____

Thinking it through . . .

1. Are you surprised that Pharaoh and his army pursued the Israelites? What implications for Egypt came with the exodus of the Israelites?

2. As God does the fighting, what seems to be important for His people?

3. Do you see significance in the cloud moving behind the Israelites during this pursuit?

_____

_____

_____

_____

_____

_____

_____

_____

_____

The Church: Key Concept

1. Read Romans 16:20. How will our battle with sin end?

2. Read Psalm 18:6-15. What is God's reaction to David's cry for help?

3. Read 2 Timothy 4:17-18. What was Timothy's assurance in spite of evil and turmoil?

_____

_____

_____

_____

_____

_____

_____

_____

_____

Thinking it through . . .

1. Are you confident that the battle you are currently facing will end in victory?
   Why or why not?

2. How do you envision God responding when you cry for help? If you had to act out His response in a game of charades, what would it look like?

3. Do you have a rock-solid assurance that God loves you like crazy and is fiercely protective of you?

_____

_____

_____

_____

_____

_____

_____

_____

LIFE LESSON 15
It's time to rejoice!

Every parent identifies with the joy of anticipation. We buy a Christmas present for one of our kids, and we get giddy every time we think of just how excited they'll be when they see it on Christmas morning. We plan a trip to Disney World, and much of the fun for us is watching our kids count down the days until our departure.

We are less inclined to rejoice, however, when we are the ones who have to wait. "I'll be able to relax when . . ." we say, though—not surprisingly—we never seem to relax whenever "when" happens. "If my husband would just . . . then, I could . . ." we negotiate. "I'll be happy when . . ." is another promise we make in vain as we grumble about our surroundings.

It's not only okay to sing now—right in the middle of your mess—but it's also appropriate. As God fights for us and leads us down the road of recovery, how can we not offer Him affection along the way? Sometimes this affection is a, "Thank you, Lord." Sometimes it's an "I love you, Lord." And sometimes, when we are especially weak, all we can offer is "Lord, you ARE God."

Moses got this. So did the Hebrew women. They had certainly not "arrived" yet; the promised land was still far away, and many struggles were yet to come before they would inherit the land. But the second the Israelites were out of firing range of the Egyptians, Moses paused to sing. The women danced. The people joined in the rejoicing. God has won! they sang. After 430 years of slavery, I imagine that this song raised the roof!

But I'm not seeing victory, you think. *I'll praise God when He answers my prayer*, or *I'll thank God once I see all the pieces put together.*

Oh, how I understand this logic. I want my way, or I want hope of a better way; I put blinders on until I see it. But in moments of miraculous usurping of my selfishness, I have been able to worship in the middle of mayhem. I can imagine God gets giddy when I do this because He loves my hugs, but He also knows the gift I will unwrap at the appointed time, so to speak. And when I crawl down from His lap to face the day again, somehow I feel a little bit taller.

Most of your life will be spent *en route*. How lonely it would feel to wait until you arrive at our Promised Land to know the comfort of Christ!

Now is the time. Right in the middle of your pain. *Rejoice!*

The Nation of Israel: Key Concepts

Read Exodus 15 as you identify these key concepts.

1. How does Moses describe the Lord in Exodus 15:3?

2. What mental picture does Moses create of God in Exodus 15:8?

3. Why did God spare the Israelites and destroy the Egyptian army? (Exodus 15:13)

4. What physical need did the people experience immediately after they worshiped? (Exodus 15:22)

5. What was discouraging when they finally found water? (Exodus 15:23)

6. As the Israelites drank the water that God had sweetened for them, what promise did He make to them? (Exodus 15:26)

_____

_____

_____

_____

_____

_____

_____

_____

_____

Thinking it through . . .

1. If you were writing a song of worship to God, how would you describe Him?

2. How do you think the Israelites felt when they finally found water and it was bitter?

3. What foundation does God establish for His laws through this experience?

_____

_____

_____

_____

_____

EXODUS: LESSONS AS YOU LEAVE

_____

_____

_____

_____

The Church: Key Concepts

1. What are we urged to do in Hebrews 12:28-29? For what can we be grateful, according to this passage?

2. Read 2 Corinthians 1:3-4. What might be the purpose of some of the bitter waters that we drink?

_____

_____

_____

_____

_____

_____

_____

_____

_____

Thinking it through . . .

1. Why is it so hard to worship in the middle of hard times?

2. When you aren't seeing victory, with what can you fill your worship?

3. How does God want us to worship Him?

4. Have you ever found "bitter waters" immediately after a season of worship? What does that do to your spirit?

5. In what ways does God sweeten your bitter waters today?

_____

LIFE LESSON 16
You need God—every day.

I wish the exodus had skipped the wilderness. After such a miraculous and long-awaited deliverance from Egyptian slavery, wouldn't it have been amazing for the Israelites to just walk straight into the land of promise? They'd suffered enough. It seems only right that they would be able to enjoy peace, plenty, and prosperity for a while, right?

God, naturally, had other plans.

The Israelites walked out of slavery into a wilderness (named "Sin," of all things) of fear and hunger. *Seriously, God? Haven't they been through enough already?* I admit my shallow, feeble thinking. I confess that sometimes the only way I can envision God's goodness is for Him to take me *out* of pain. Heal my child of this illness, Lord. Provide my husband another job, Lord. Help me lose weight, Lord.

These aren't wrong prayers at all, but they do make me realize that my expectation for God's intervention rarely involves my staying in pain. I pray for the finished product that I want, and when it doesn't come right away, I stifle a groan out of obligatory faithfulness to be content in whatsoever state I'm in, as the apostle Paul would say.

Right now I'm praying for a sister in Christ to be healed of an insatiable cancer. With four young children and a loving husband, her battle here on earth is almost over, and it makes me sick with grief. *She's only 38 years old, Lord. Please, please heal her!* Having to surrender to hospice care seemed like a cruel playground prank in a recess that never ended.

I'm starting to see, however, that God's love is bigger than our myopic view of life. I'm thinking that the Israelites were learning this, too. *We should have just stayed in slavery! At least in Egypt we weren't hungry! Or maybe, Way to roll, Moses. God leads us out and then leaves us for dead here in the middle of nowhere.* Just like I just want God to take this sweet woman and her family out of this pain and make her 100 percent well again here on earth, the Israelites seemed similarly narrow-minded. Just like me, they forgot to anticipate the journey between slavery and freedom.

The journey, however, is where God nurses us. One day at a time. One crisis at a time. One prayer at a time. Contrary to what our society promotes in the "self-made man" or the "independent woman," God wants us completely reliant on Him. Some of the Israelites were greedy for material security; they disobeyed God and tried to save up manna to have as surplus. When we try to stockpile faith so that we can skip daily interaction with God, we, too, end up feeling abandoned by God.

Don't wait until Sunday to worship God. Don't wait until your quiet time to pray. Don't wait until you hear a cool song on Christian radio to sing. You need God right now.

The Nation of Israel: Key Concepts

Read Exodus 16 as you identify these key concepts.

1. Why did the Israelites wish they were back in Egypt? (Exodus 16:3)

2. Why does God plan to give food to the people of Israel one day at a time? (Exodus 16:4)

3. Where did the glory of the Lord appear in the wilderness? (Exodus 16:10)

4. What did the people eat at night? (Exodus 16:13) What did they eat in the mornings? (Exodus 16:15)

5. What happened when the people tried to store up extra manna before the sixth day of the week? (Exodus 16:20)

6. How long did the nation of Israel eat manna from the Lord? (Exodus 16:35)

Thinking it through . . .

1. After all the torture they had experienced during slavery, why do you think the Israelites were grumbling about hunger?

2. What can we learn about how God rationed out food one day at a time?

3. Why do you think God wanted them not to gather on the Sabbath?

4. What do you imagine their feelings were like after eating the same food every day for decades?

_____

_____

_____

_____

_____

_____

_____

_____

The Church: Key Concepts

1. What does Jesus call Himself in John 6:35?

2. How often are we to pray for this Bread? (Matthew 6:11)

3. What does "Sabbath rest" mean for today's Christians? (Hebrews 4:9-10)

_____

_____

_____

_____

_____

_____

_____

_____

Thinking it through . . .

1. Do your prayers reflect a daily reliance on God, or do you pray mostly for one-time answers?

2. Does your life and your walk with Christ demonstrate a daily reliance on God?

3. Have you "rested from your works" and entered the rest of God?

4. Is it hard for you to leave bondage only to go into more hardship? How do you see God in this?

_____

_____

_____

_____

_____

_____

_____

_____

LIFE LESSON 17
We must support fellow Christians in battle.

My husband and I keep our kids on a tight leash in terms of space in our house. They aren't allowed to shut doors (except when using the bathroom), and their electronics stay in our room at night. As much as we crave reprieve through the exhaustion of parenting, we don't want our boys to be outside of our earshot or sight range. Even though electronics in their bedroom might give us uninterrupted time at night, we don't want them choosing what noise puts them to sleep.

Controlling? No. This isn't a punitive measure. It's our way of proactively putting a rock beneath them when they start to get spiritually weary. Solitude and privacy are petri dishes for temptation, and we want to control the temperature in the laboratory of sin that seeks to destroy our boys.

If your eyebrows are raised, take a minute and look at Exodus 17. Israel fights their first battle after leaving Egypt. As Joshua leads the charge against the Amalekites, Moses, Aaron, and Hur go to battle in prayer. Not long into the battle, Moses sees a connection between his uplifted arms and the victory of the Israelites. If this weren't a spiritual battle as well, he might have even been tempted to have a little fun with his new Inspector Gadget arms. *Clap on. Clap off. Clap on, clap off*—ok, anyway, the bad part was that Moses's circulation was no stronger than ours. In other words, he got tired.

Try this rock, Aaron and Hur said, while perhaps privately trying out their own arms in envy. Moses sits down, and Aaron and Hur resort to propping his arms up so that the Israelites can finish the job with the Amalekites.

So back to our house rules. One day, our kids are going to be tempted to watch something they shouldn't. One day Satan is going to try to swallow them with loneliness or depression. One day we're all going to be too tired to do family. But that won't exactly be an option because . . . well, we're tucked in pretty tightly in our nest, and nobody gets to check out of the family environment. Right now, then, we see our rules as the prop we will each need when our spiritual battles become long and tiring. We stay close in proximity to one another so that we can hold one another's arms up.

Our responsibility is first to our family members, then to the family of God. Rather than judge fellow Christians (including members of our household) who are losing a battle, we must crawl under them and hold them up. Rather than gossip about struggling believers or grumbling about the failures of our husbands or children, we are called by God to give them what they need to win the battle.

Go, go Gadget arms!

The Nation of Israel: Key Concepts

Read Exodus 17 as you identify these key concepts.

1. Before the battle with the Amalekites, what bizarre miracle does God perform to meet the Israelites' needs? (Exodus 17:6)

2. What does Moses carry up to the hill with him? (Exodus 17:9)

3. What happened when Moses's hands were raised? What happened when they were lowered? (Exodus 17:11)

4. What name does Moses give God after the victory? (Exodus 17:15)

_____

_____

_____

_____

_____

_____

_____

_____

Thinking it through . . .

1. What do you make of the Lord's bringing water out of a *rock*?

2. Why do you think Moses's staff is significant?

3. What seems to be important to God after this victory?

4. Do you think Aaron and Hur went up the hill expecting to have to hold Moses up?

_____

_____

_____

_____

_____

_____

_____

_____

_____

The Church: Key Concepts

1. What does Scripture urge us to do with respect to fellow believers? (Galatians 6:1-2)

2. What is the "sword of the Spirit"? (Ephesians 6:17)

3. What are we to do all the time, on behalf of fellow believers? (Ephesians 6:18)

_____

_____

_____

_____

_____

_____

_____

_____

Thinking it through . . .

1. Take a close look at your heart. When someone in your household is struggling, is your first instinct to criticize or to pray? Do you get angry, or do you help?

2. Answer the same question about your heart toward fellow believers.

3. Is there a difference in how you respond to your own family versus how you respond to other believers?

4. Why did Noah build the ark? (Whom was he trying to save?)

5. Where should our support for believers begin?

6. Do you think there is a connection between Moses's staff and the "sword of the Spirit"? If so, what does this mean about our conduct in battle?

_____

_____

_____

_____

_____

_____

_____

_____

God Leaves Little to the Imagination
(EXODUS 18-20)

LIFE LESSON 18
Honor counsel from the wise.

*W*ait. If there was any word I hated to hear more from my mother while growing up, then I surely can't remember it. Creative and sometimes impulsive, I would often see an item in a catalog or in a store and beg my mother to let me buy it. Her answer was nearly always, *Wait*. Sometimes it was for practical reasons—wait until you have enough money or wait until we see if you will actually need this. Other times, though, I think my mother knew that if I waited even ten minutes, I might not want or need this item enough to think about it again.

Oh how I hated to hear her say that word, but as an adult, I realize that *waiting* is one of the most valuable lessons my mother ever taught me. When I have a big decision to make, I now force myself to wait through at least one night of good rest so that I never make an important judgment call when I'm tired. When shopping for a larger item, such as a piece of furniture or a vehicle, I often walk away—*wait*—and then go back the next day if I'm still sure I want it. And—Lord, help them—the one word my children hear from me often enough to hate it, too, is *wait*.

What advice did your parents give you often as you grew up? What was your reaction to it? Do you now see the wisdom in it? Often I have noticed myself preferring the advice I get from my female friends, especially when they affirm my right to gripe or complain. No doubt my friends love me, but Exodus 18 reminds me of who often has more of our best interests at heart—our family members.

As we wrestle with our newfound freedom in Christ—whether it be the freedom from damnation that comes when we are born into Christ or the freedoms we encounter as we "lay aside every weight and sin" (Hebrews 12:1), we will need counsel. We need mentors. We need people to show us the ways of righteous, responsible living. How we respond to advice when we receive it says a lot about us and our commitment to holiness—especially when that advice comes from a family member.

The Nation of Israel: Key Concepts

Read Exodus 18 as you identify these key concepts.

1. How do Moses and his father-in-law begin their conversation? (Exodus 18:7)

2. What revelation did their conversation bring about for Jethro? (Exodus 18:11)

3. Judging by Exodus 18:14, where does it appear that Jethro was while Moses was judging the people?

4. Summarize Jethro's concern. (Exodus 18:17-18)

5. What is Jethro's advice to Moses? (Exodus 18:21)

6. What is Moses's response? (Exodus 18:24)

_____

_____

_____

_____

_____

_____

_____

_____

_____

Thinking it through . . .

1. What can we infer about the kind of relationship Moses had with his father-in-law?

2. What kind of spiritual breakthrough did this experience bring about for Jethro?

3. What do you think Moses was thinking when his father-in-law told him that he was doing things all wrong?

4. What do you think Jethro's heart was behind all this?

_____

_____

_____

_____

_____

_____

_____

_____

_____

The Church: Key Concepts

1. Read Proverbs 13:20. What is the principle in this verse?

2. Read 2 Timothy 3:2-5. What are characteristics of people who often appear to be churchgoing, God-fearing individuals but who are actually spitting in the face of God?

3. Read 1 Timothy 2:11. How is a woman to learn the ways of God?

_____

_____

_____

_____

_____

_____

_____

_____

Thinking it through . . .

1. From whom do we often seek advice when going through difficult times?

2. What role do our parents (including in-laws) play in our lives as adults?

3. Is it easier for you to accept advice and counsel from someone outside your household? Do you get irritated when your husband gives you advice?

4. Why is it important to honor the advice we receive during our exodus, especially the advice that comes from parents and spouses?

5. What if a spouse or parent gives ungodly advice? Is it possible to still honor them? Where would God want you to seek advice if you can't get it from your family?

LIFE LESSON 19

Sometimes He comes in the clouds.

When my younger son was just a few weeks old, I sat one chilly January day at the kitchen table and nursed him while Drew, my then-almost-three-year-old, played on the floor with his LEGOs®. We had cabin fever, as it was winter and I was just starting to feel human again after giving birth. As I fed Jack, Drew begged to go outside. Though it was cold and yucky out, I gave in—with one condition.

"We can go outside after Mommy's done feeding Jack, but you'll have to pick up your Legos first," I said. Drew looked at the disaster around his feet and pleaded not to have to pick up his toys.

"But, Mama, it's so hard. There's so many of them."

Smiling, I saw my opportunity to weave in a spiritual lesson. "When something is hard, honey, you should pray and ask Jesus to help you."

Drew dropped to the floor and was silent for a moment. Then, his little head popped up and he reported matter-of-factly, "I prayed. He said He'd do it Himself."

I've told this story many times whenever I've been in circles where moms start sharing all the funny things their kids have said and done. Though I found it hard to explain to Drew why God wouldn't pick up his Legos for him, I marveled at his eagerness to pray in an overwhelming situation.

Sometimes, it's these overwhelming situations that get our attention. We see our smallness, our powerlessness, and we recognize that we need God. Admittedly, the sweetest seasons of my walk with Christ have directly coincided with hardship. Losing a much-wanted baby enabled me to feel the skin of Jesus through the endless hugs of sisters in Christ. My divorce from my children's biological father and its horrible aftermath brought me to a level of dependency on Christ that I'd never known before. Oh, how I hate these moments of intense grief and heartache, but I crave the intimacy with God that inevitably results from tragedy.

The pattern in Scripture seems to be that God doesn't show up how we expect Him. In this lesson, He shows up in a cloud because He wants to be sure He gets the Israelites' attention . *Lord, you've scared the bejeebers out of them*, Moses must have been thinking when God shook Mount Sinai like it was a snow globe. But God wouldn't let them off the hook. He had an invitation—a calling to be His people—and He wanted everyone to attend the party.

Is it possible, then, that the same cloud that is bringing you down and sucking the joy out of you also contains a message to draw near to God?

Actually, this cloud quite possibly contains God Himself.

The Nation of Israel: Key Concepts

Read Exodus 19 as you identify these key concepts.

1. When the Israelites reached the wilderness of Sinai, how did God call to Moses? (Exodus 19:3)

2. How was God planning to come to the Israelites? (Exodus 19:9)

3. Why was God planning to come this way? (Exodus 19:9)

4. When Moses speaks to God, how does God answer? (Exodus 19:19)

_____

_____

_____

_____

_____

_____

_____

_____

Thinking it through . . .

1. Imagine that you had been one of the Israelites in Sinai. What would your reaction have been to God's appearance?

2. Do you think the Israelites recognized that this was God? Why or why not?

3. When royalty or other high-ranking officials make an appearance somewhere, how do they typically show up?

4. Does God seem to follow that pattern?

5. What are your thoughts about God's coming in a cloud?

_____

_____

_____

_____

_____

_____

_____

_____

_____

The Church: Key Concepts

1. How will Jesus return to earth one day? (Luke 21:27)

2. What kind of "clouds" had Paul experienced? (2 Corinthians 11:24-28)

3. What was Paul's response to this? (2 Corinthians 12:1)

4. What should our response to suffering be? (1 Peter 4:13)

_____

_____

_____

_____

_____

_____

_____

_____

_____

Thinking it through . . .

1. Why do you think we have a tendency to equate clouds with suffering and hardship?

2. When are clouds a good thing?

3. Can we learn anything about the pattern of God's appearing in clouds?

4. Why might God choose to visit us, so to speak, in a cloud?

_____

_____

_____

_____

_____

_____

_____

_____

LIFE LESSON 20
There are rules for holy living.

My classroom teaching background has ingrained in me one cardinal rule for classroom management: Post a list of rules. Contrary to what some may think, kids actually *want* to do the right thing most of the time. Classroom management problems most commonly arise *not* because kids are rebellious and ornery; rather, frantic moments and disciplinary issues are usually the result of the kids' simply not knowing what to do. They don't know the rules when a substitute is present, for example. Or they don't know the procedure for sharpening a pencil that breaks in the middle of a test. Or they don't know what they are supposed to do once they 'get into groups of four.'

So the sermon I preach in nearly every class I teach to aspiring teachers is to develop and teach clear rules and procedures and to consistently give clear task directions in more than one format. Amazingly, this makes a huge difference in how a classroom runs from bell-to-bell.

This principle is nothing new. God had seen the Israelites pledge their loyalty to Him—they wanted to follow Him and do what was pleasing to Him. God also knew that they would likely develop myriad versions of what righteous living looked like unless He gave them specific rules Himself.

We know them as the Ten Commandments. We've colored pictures in Sunday School of a long-bearded crazy man holding up stone tablets the shape of McDonalds arches, and we've faithfully memorized the list of rules on those stones.

Sometimes following Christ is as simple as obedience. We often whine at how we just wish we knew what God would have us to do. For starters, let's remind ourselves of the basic rules for holy living. With the exception of keeping a Sabbath day (see Hebrews 4 for the rest we experience under the new covenant), the New Testament reinforces all of the Ten Commandments in some fashion.

We'd like to justify why we can't honor our parents. We may have a good explanation for why we lied. But the bottom line is this: There are rules for holy living. We can't rationalize sin, and we are not exempt from punishment if we try.

The Nation of Israel: Key Concepts

Read Exodus 20 as you identify these key concepts.

1. How does God describe Himself in Exodus 20:5?

2. What is His promise to those who keep His commandments? (Exodus 19:6)

3. As a reminder, write out the Ten Commandments. (Exodus 19:7-17)

_____

_____

_____

_____

_____

_____

_____

_____

Thinking it through . . .

1. What are your thoughts on the jealousy of God?

2. When did you first encounter the Ten Commandments?

3. Do you tend to see the Ten Commandments as outdated and only relevant for the Israelites?

_____

_____

_____

_____

_____

_____

_____

_____

The Church: Key Concepts

* Spend a few moments finding reinforcement in the New Testament for each of the Ten Commandments. Use Hebrews 4 to address the commandment about the Sabbath. For the other references, use your concordance, or use an Internet search engine to help you. Record the references for each commandment.

_____

_____

_____

_____

_____

_____

_____

_____

_____

_____

_____

_____

_____

_____

_____

_____

_____

Thinking it through . . .

1. What are the hardest rules to follow as Christians in today's world?

2. When are we prone to try to rationalize sin?

3. Do we value these rules appropriately? In other words, do we overemphasize them and leave out grace? Or do we disregard them and promote a cheapness of grace that spurns the holiness of God?

_____

_____

_____

_____

_____

_____

_____

_____

SESSION 7

God Won't Leave Us to Our Own Devices
(EXODUS 21-24)

LIFE LESSON 21
How you treat people matters.

L et's face it, ladies. Some days we just don't feel it. Whether our bad mood is dressed in hormones or otherwise justified by life's relentless mayhem, I'll bet we all can easily recall a day or two when we just gave into our feelings and lowered our expectations for ourselves that day. "It's that time of the month" or "I haven't had my caffeine yet" become our disclaimers when others raise their eyebrows at our rudeness or crankiness.

Perhaps we've even compartmentalized our holiness. An especially demanding boss or a pretentious, showy friend have bankrupted our bank of compassion, and we no longer try to be Christ-like when we are at work or in a particular social circle. A family member hurts us over and over and over again—never apologizes, yet holds grand expectations from us. Surely there are limits to the extent to which we are expected to be nice to people, right?

Facebook is full of memes, advice, and inspiring quotes. One idea I've seen several times in the last few weeks—and I'm paraphrasing here—is to "get rid of people (I assume this means to sever relationships with these people, as opposed to providing endless fodder for future "Dateline" episodes) who discourage you or otherwise bring negativity into your life." Although I see the wisdom in boundaries and choosing close friends wisely, I'm not sure righteous living entitles us to simply dismiss annoying, irritating, or coldhearted people. Exodus 21 gives directives for how the Israelites are to treat one another, especially in situations where they've stepped on one another's toes. Anticipating they might have carried some emotional baggage out of Egypt along with jewels and livestock, God immediately follows the Big 10 (Exodus 20) with specific directions for keeping things right among people who had only recently escaped a lifetime of abuse. If they were going to last a day longer without killing one another, God knew He needed to spell out the syllabus for Relationships 101.

Maybe your heart is heavy right now because you, too, have been the victim of physical, sexual, or emotional abuse. Getting out of the abusive situation was hard enough, but healing has been a predictable mixture of progress and pain. Research suggests that victims of abuse often become abusers themselves without constructive intervention and recovery. You grew up under a harsh hand, so you are raising your children the same way. You were molested as a teenager by an older cousin, who, as it turns out, had been abused by his own father. The cycle of abuse has continued, and you hate yourself for it.

Fortunately, God is quite clear about His expectations. We don't have to try to figure things out on our own when it comes to pleasing Him in how we treat people. The Israelites were broken and angry and afraid, so God wasn't going to gamble on their knowing proper ways to treat one another. Similarly, the New Covenant outlines God's expectations for us, for we, too, are a broken people. Were we not bathed in the blood of Jesus, we could never endure the painful exodus from our secret places.

Making a change in how we treat people is as simple as obedience. We cannot—hear this—CANNOT wait for warm feelings to arrive. We are told to be kind to one another (Ephesians 4:32; Colossians 3:12), so we must simply obey whether we feel like it or not. How we treat people matters to God, and we cannot allow ourselves to get away with sin simply because we left the house too late to run through Starbucks.

God had a passionate plan to heal the Israelites (2 Chronicles 7:14), but healing was contingent upon obedience. Obey God now so that your exodus doesn't turn into a futile, dead-end road trip.

The Nation of Israel: Key Concepts
Read Exodus 21 as you identify these key concepts.

1. What did God require Israelites to do for their servants every seven years? (Exodus 21:2)

2. What did God expect from a murderer? What about from someone who killed by accident? (Exodus 21:12-14)

3. How did God feel about sin toward one's parents? (Exodus 21:15, 17)

4. Read the remaining verses, and list a few more guidelines God gives for certain wrongs among people.

_____

_____

_____

_____

_____

_____

_____

_____

Thinking it through . . .

1. What do these guidelines tell us about God's heart for people who are powerless—people who are victimized by another's wrongdoing?

2. How do you think God is defining "fair" here?

3. Why do you think God demands a harsher punishment for sin against one's parents?

_____

_____

_____

_____

_____

_____

_____

_____

The Church: Key Concepts

1. What three things did God promise to do for the Israelites in exchange for their obedience? (2 Chronicles 7:14)

2. How would Christ have us to think of one another? (Philippians 2:3)

3. What law are we to follow now in our relationships with other people? (Galatians 5:14)

4. Specifically, what does this look like? (Ephesians 4:32)

_____

_____

_____

_____

_____

_____

_____

_____

_____

_____

_____

_____

_____

_____

_____

Thinking it through . . .

1. How do God's ways contrast with the advice we get from others sometimes?

2. Talk about the paradigm shift that is required for us to think of kindness, compassion, forgiveness, etc. as acts of obedience instead of acts born from feelings.

3. Take an honest look at your ways of relating to others, including people in your family, your social circle, your workplace, and your church. Where are you being disobedient to the law of Christ?

_____

_____

_____

_____

_____

_____

LIFE LESSON 22
Right is right.

I think the time has come for us to pause and take a hard, honest look at sin. I'm not talking about the Big Ones: adultery, murder, or cursing the name of the Lord. If you've spent even five minutes in church, you've probably graded yourself on how well you avoid the Big Ones. As some have proudly said, "We don't smoke, and we don't chew, and we don't go with boys who do." Confident in our ability to walk the straight and narrow, we see our Christian walk as the opportunity to learn more of God's Word and to do more good works. We've checked the Big Ones off the list of things to worry about, so it's like we no longer ponder the cumbersome presence of sin in our lives. Repudiating sin, however, is the foundation of our Christian walk. We cannot become like Jesus if we remain hospitable to sin.

In Exodus 22, God seems to be addressing the sins that are easily hidden or even justified. Indeed, some of the sins God condemns in this chapter are those which are often justified in culture. Premarital sex. Sorcery. Necrophilia. Idolatry. Cruelty to foreigners. Taking advantage of vulnerable groups of people. Usery. Contempt for a leader. Greed. Laziness. (See verses 16-31)

Are you uncomfortable yet? I sure am. I am 100 percent sure that I have entertained a few idols. I am 100 percent sure that I have badmouthed someone in authority over me. I could go on, but you get the idea. In fact, you might be thinking, *But this is a nonissue. We live under the New Covenant. These laws don't apply to us anymore.*

You're right. But you're also wrong. Sin is still sin. What has changed is how sin is atoned for. God no longer commands us to put to death anyone who practices sorcery. But is sorcery still a sin? *You bet!* Revelation 21:8 and Galatians 5:19-21 condemn the same sins mentioned in Exodus 22. Sin is sin, and no matter how relevant or essential it appears in our culture, God hates it, and He holds your soul accountable for it.

So back to our look in the mirror. Where in our lives do we see idols? Sure, they may not be 24-karat gold cows as the centerpieces in our dining room, but do they take the form of a substitute-God? (See Exodus 32—idols are what we look to when God doesn't appear to be showing up or when we are tired of waiting on God.) Where in our lives do we allow the influence of the demonic world? (Challenge me if you want, but decorating our homes with witches and ghosts every October dances a whole lot closer to the subject of God's hatred than I want to be.) Where in our lives do we endorse premarital sex? (Maybe on our favorite TV shows?) Where in our lives do we show contempt for others? (No explanation needed!)

Both the Old and New Covenants give us a plenteous list of sins to avoid. If we are finding our exodus at a standstill, perhaps we need to revisit sin in our lives—specifically, the sins that we aren't too worried about. The sins that are clothed in justification. The sins that aren't easy to spot.

Right is right. We may be pilgrims on a journey to the raw heart of God, but we will never be welcome at His table if we insist on casually dating sin on the side.

The Nation of Israel: Key Concepts

Read Exodus 22 as you identify these key concepts.

1. What was God's perspective on how the Israelites were to repay people they had wronged? (Exodus 22: 1, 4, 9, 14, etc.)

2. What heading (if any) does your Bible give to Exodus 22: 16-31?

3. How is God's mercy and compassion evident, even in the punishment of these sins? (Exodus 22: 23-24, 26-27)

_____

_____

_____

_____

_____

_____

_____

_____

Thinking it through . . .

1. What seems different about the sins that are to be punished with death, versus the sins that are to be atoned through financial compensation?

2. What groups of people does God seem to defend with a passion?

3. What sinful tendency might God be addressing in Exodus 22:31?
(Exodus 22:23-24, 26-27)

_____

_____

_____

_____

_____

_____

_____

_____

_____

The Church: Key Concepts

1. Read Galatians 5:19-21. List all of the sins mentioned in these verses.

2. What was one action taken by new believers in Ephesus when they saw the controlling, oppressive power of a demonic spirit? (See Acts 19:16 and 19:19.)

3. Did God retain His soft spot for vulnerable, weak groups of people when the New Covenant was enacted? (See Matthew 25:35-40.) (Exodus 22: 23-24, 26-27)

_____

_____

_____

_____

_____

_____

_____

_____

_____

_____

_____

_____

_____

_____

_____

_____

Thinking it through . . .

1. What sins are present in your life on a regular basis? Are you justifying them, or are you actively turning from them?

2. What are ways we unknowingly endorse sin? What would God have us do in these cases?

3. Reflect on your relationship with your earthly father. What does it mean to you that God adamantly defends the fatherless and the orphans?

4. Is it hard for you to accept the harsh punishment for unrepented sins but, at the same time, fully grasp God's tender heart of compassion?

_____

_____

_____

_____

_____

_____

_____

_____

_____

LIFE LESSON 23
Baby steps aren't "maybe" steps.

Have you ever received joyous news like the excitement of a small child at Christmas, only later to have your euphoria eclipsed by some fine print? As I write this, the national lottery value is over a billion dollars. A billion dollars! If someone (or more than one "someone") actually wins this week, I imagine that that person will be in a merry stupor for at least a little while. My guess is that before the jumping balls in the big plastic vacuum box even return to inertia, this money will be spent in the mind of the winner(s).

Whoever wins, however, needs to keep some not-so-fun news in mind as they grab their checkbook and head to the luxury car lot. In one word: taxes. I have no idea what taxes on a billion plus sum would be, but I am sure that the net payout will be slightly less exciting than the initial value. The winner will not be a billionaire, as he or she currently may hope to be. Alas, the final fortune will *only* be in the millions.

I'm guessing that this might disappoint the winner. Maybe not—maybe I'm wrong—but the greedy, entitled souls we all war against daily will likely grab the winner's earlobe and whisper in it sweet nothings of what "a billion" could have enabled them to do, versus "just several million."

Exodus 23 might be the fine print on the deed to the Promised Land that God had gifted to Israel. I'm not sure the Hebrew men and women counted on their new home being occupied when they got there. Imagine inheriting a vast estate after years of struggle that included homelessness, abuse, and despair . . . only to find out that this turn key operation probably wasn't going to go down smoothly. Your enemies occupy the estate, and they haven't even started packing for their move out.

When I read verses 20-33, I can picture their eyes gradually getting wider. Pupils fully dilated, perhaps they start whispering among themselves, "Moses didn't say anything about this part." To add to their anxiety, God then informs them that He thinks it's best to drive out the enemies "little by little" (verse 30) instead of in one fell swoop. God wants to protect them from just being taken right back over (this time by wild animals—see verse 29), so His plan gives them time to increase in number and build up the land.

You can probably picture an instance when God didn't answer your prayers all at once. Or maybe He answered them they way you'd hoped, but the accompanying responsibilities aren't quite what you bargained for. We ache for quick fixes in our lives—a miracle diet to reach our dreamed-of weight, a winning lottery ticket to solve our financial problems, or a big shiny SUV to satisfy our hunger for something trendy and material. Experts say, however, that lasting results—be they pounds of fat or peace of mind—aren't typically the result of quick fixes. We all know this, of course, but we hate the honest truth that the most sincere victories are won little by little.

Little by little. Maybe some of the Israelites were angry with God. Maybe some of them felt duped and were enraged at the news that they'd have to eat this elephant one bite at a time. *How dare God make a promise but then tell us He couldn't give it to us all at once?* Maybe they felt betrayed and were unsure that God would indeed give them what He said He would.

We know now God's logic and wisdom in not handing over the keys to the Promised Land all at once. But, at the time, His chosen beloved people didn't have the whole story in front of them. They couldn't scroll down a ways and see their descendants march into victory. They couldn't see that baby steps did not mean maybe steps.

If you're standing at that same moment of uncertainty about God, don't turn around and go back. Breathe in the loving, compassionate heart of your God, and trust Him with your next steps.

The Nation of Israel: Key Concepts
Read Exodus 23 as you identify these key concepts.

1. As God finishes giving directives for holy living among one another, what evidence do we see about His tender, gentle heart? (Exodus 23:5, 11, 12)

2. What did God put in place to ensure the Israelites' protection? (Exodus 23:20)

3. Examine Exodus 23:23-26. What condition did God set for His blessings?

_____

_____

_____

_____

_____

_____

_____

_____

_____

Thinking it through . . .

1. Why do you think God emphasizes obedience to the angel who will go before the Israelites?

2. Imagine you were one of the Hebrews who heard God say that He would drive out your enemies "little by little." What would you feel at that moment? What would your response to God be?

3. Do you ever feel yourself crying out "that's not fair" to God's ways? Process that, not being afraid to be raw and honest about what these moments are like for you.

_____

_____

_____

_____

_____

_____

_____

_____

The Church: Key Concepts

1. Read Revelation 1:5-6. What has Christ done for us?

2. Read James 1:12. What is the condition set for receiving God's promise?

3. Read 1 Thessalonians 5:24. What does this verse tell us about God?

_____

_____

_____

_____

_____

_____

_____

_____

_____

_____

_____

_____

_____

_____

_____

_____

_____

Thinking it through . . .

1. Do you spend more time thinking about what you want or seeking out what God wants? How does this affect your faith in God during difficult times?

2. How patient are you during hardship? Do you feel tempted to seek out idols or to run back into a bondage situation?

3. At this exact moment—today, right now—how do you view God's character? How do you view His ability to safeguard you?

_____

_____

_____

_____

_____

_____

_____

_____

LIFE LESSON 24
Come up to the Lord.

My second-favorite movie of all time includes a heartwarming exchange between a powerful king and his tiny, young daughter. In *Anna and the King*, the ways of royalty and the privilege of position in the palace of King Mongkut of Siam are known well by all. Not even the king's personal assistant approaches Mongkut's throne without bowing and being granted permission to speak. Many are never even allowed to get off their knees in the presence of this king.

In this scene, however, a tender irony ensues when the king's favorite child (of his 40+ children), nicknamed "Monkey," needs her daddy. In a tense throne room with a handful of high-ranking generals, King Mongkut agonizes over ominous threats to his country and his heirs. Smack dab in the middle of this secret meeting, the towering doors at the far end of the throne room open clumsily as a tiny little Monkey squeezes through and runs full tilt down the length of the room. Her bare feet patter lightly on the posh red carpet, and she unabashedly shoves past the dignitaries who are, incidentally, prostrate again since a princess has entered.

Monkey climbs up to Mongkut's seat with impressive agility, not slowing down until she's cradled in his lap. Whatever imminent danger the country of Siam is in is temporarily forgotten by Mongkut, who has bent his ear to Monkey's lips. At this moment, her little voice and whatever she's tattletaling about are all he hears. He scoops her up to his large shoulders and leaves the throne room to see what all her fuss is about.

Come up to the Lord, God commands Moses in Exodus 24. Elders and leaders will go with him, but only to a point. It's Moses and Moses alone with whom God wants to speak. *Moses alone shall come near to the Lord*, verse 2 reads. I'm thinking this might have made Moses a tad nervous. God wasn't inviting him to meet at Baskin Robbins and talk over a waffle cone; instead, Moses had to ascend a mountain encased in a cloud.

Um, M-Moses? This is creepy! his assistant Joshua may have whispered as they inched their way up blindly. *In fact, it's getting a bit warm—yikes! Is that fire up there??* This isn't Moses's first rodeo, though, and he has grown accustomed to God's impressive disguises. I can imagine Moses shushing Joshua, telling him to wait here, and then proceeding on with a confident grip on his staff—a souvenir to which he's grown a bit attached ever since it devoured inferior serpents in Pharoah's court.

Moses entered the cloud, Scripture states (verse 18). Like Monkey from *Anna and the King*, Moses entered his Creator's presence with confidence in the relationship they had with each other. No arguing this time. No begging God to pick someone else. No pointing to his mouth to remind God of his speech impediment. Instead, Moses simply enters God's presence, undeterred by the weather forecast.

If you are a daughter of our great King Jesus, you have an open invitation to enter His throne room. You don't have to ask permission. You don't have to dress nicely and clean up your act first.

Jesus died *while we were yet sinners* (Romans 5:8). He didn't wait until we got over it. Fellow traveler, stop this moment and *go near to your God.*

The Nation of Israel: Key Concepts

Read Exodus 24 as you identify these key concepts.

1. Whom did God call up to Himself? (Exodus 24:1) What was different about God's directions for Moses? (Exodus 24:2)
2. What did Moses do with the words of the Lord? (Exodus 24:4)
3. Describe the initial meeting between God and the Hebrew leaders. (Exodus 24:9-11)
4. What covered the mountain where God was? (Exodus 24:15)
   What covered the top of the mountain where the glory of the Lord was? (Exodus 24:17)

_____

_____

_____

_____

_____

_____

_____

_____

_____

Thinking it through . . .

1. Why do you think God wanted to sequester only Moses in His presence?
2. What evidence do you see in this chapter that Moses is more confident now in God's vision for His people?
3. Why do you think God dwelled in a cloud and a fire? Why on top of a mountain?

_____

_____

_____

_____

_____

_____

_____

_____

_____

The Church: Key Concepts

1. Read Matthew 27:51. What happened to the curtain in the temple right after Jesus died?

2. Read Hebrews 4:16. How does God want us to approach His throne?

3. Read Matthew 11:28-29. What invitation does God give to those who are tired and weighed down heavily?

_____

_____

_____

_____

_____

_____

_____

_____

_____

_____

_____

_____

_____

_____

_____

_____

_____

Thinking it through . . .

1. Picture yourself as the small girl who abandons formalities, runs up to her father's throne, and crawls into her spot on his lap. Do you have a hard time leaning into this type of intimacy with God? Why or why not?

2. What is the significance of the curtain of the temple being torn? What does this mean to you personally?

3. What do you think we can learn from the tendency of God to reveal Himself to Moses and the Israelites through clouds and fire?

4. If you were literally sitting on God's lap in this physical world, right at this moment, what would you talk to Him about?

5. What tends to keep you from tenderness and intimacy in your Father-daughter relationship with God?

_____

_____

_____

_____

_____

_____

_____

_____

God Will Never Leave You Alone in the Dark

(EXODUS 25-27)

LIFE LESSON 25

Let the Lord come to you.

The whole point of the elaborate, ornate Ark of the Covenant was that God was itching to be among His people. Not content to dwell in flames from afar, God ached for closeness with His creation. He once enjoyed evening strolls with Adam in the Garden of Eden, and God now wanted communion with the people of Israel.

But that wasn't exactly possible. An ugly, malignant mastodon called *sin* created a bit of a problem. Holiness—which we will explore in a later chapter—simply cannot co-mingle with the rancid stench of rebellion, idolatry, witchcraft, deception, fornication, and so on. The time was not yet right for God's Ultimate Redemption Plan, though, so God was in a pickle: either live with a chasm between Himself and His creation for countless generations or figure out a way to live among His people but protect His holiness.

Where were the mogul investors from the hit reality series *Shark Tank* when God outlined His ingenious plan? He gave Moses directions for the Ark of the Covenant. Down to the fabric of its design, God left no room for economic shortcuts. God needed a holy place to dwell if He was to be among his loves, but Supreme Holiness couldn't be sheltered with burlap. The richest, most luxurious materials and design would be used to create a sacred, lovely place for God's presence to live.

In the midst of the architectural blueprint that forms this session, it would be easy to miss the most miraculous love driving the whole operation. "And let them make me a sanctuary," God told Moses, "that I may dwell in their midst." God wanted to be with them. He wanted to be among these sinful, tired, complaining, wandering, fickle-minded people.

And He wants to dwell with you. Sinful, tired, complaining, wandering, fickle-minded you.

Let Him come. He will change you forever.

The Nation of Israel: Key Concepts
Read Exodus 25 as you identify these key concepts.

1. Read Exodus 25:2. How were the supplies for the sanctuary acquired?
2. Once the structure was complete, from where would God speak? (Exodus 25:21, 22)
3. What would the people need to set before God regularly? (Exodus 25:30)

_____

_____

_____

_____

_____

_____

_____

_____

Thinking it through . . .

1. Why do you think God specified the supplies come from "every man whose heart moves him"?
2. What significance is there in God's speaking from the "mercy seat"?
3. Why do you think God's directions were so minute and specific?
4. Why do you think God chose *bread* as a permanent staple on the table?

_____

_____

_____

_____

_____

_____

_____

_____

The Church: Key Concepts

1. Read Matthew 1:23. How did God come to us?

2. Read Matthew 14:25-27. What did Jesus do here? How did He calm the disciples' fear?

3. Read John 4:4 as an introduction to the story of Jesus and the woman at the well. Geography aside, what does this verse suggest about Jesus' heart for that woman?

_____

_____

_____

_____

_____

_____

_____

_____

_____

_____

_____

_____

_____

_____

_____

_____

Thinking it through . . .

1. What emotion often characterized people who were approached by Jesus?

2. What emotions do you feel when you realize God wants to be near to you?

3. Search online for a New Testament map of the nation of Israel. Geographically speaking, did Jesus *have* to travel through Samaria to get from Judea to Galilee? Do you see this scene as Jesus approaching her or the woman approaching Jesus?

4. What offering does God want from you in exchange for His presence?

_____

_____

_____

_____

_____

_____

_____

_____

LIFE LESSON 26
God is holier than our holiest holy.

Have you ever met somebody famous? My husband has met several celebrities. Growing up in California probably accounts for some of this, but he also has uncanny facial recognition ability. (He should have been a CIA agent!) Often when we are in airports or restaurants, he immediately recognizes the most random people. Even behind their sunglasses and baggy disguises, no face can fool Steve's eidetic memory. And while he's definitely not a groupie, he certainly doesn't pass up a chance to get a photo and sometimes an autograph from whomever he spots.

Most famous people thrive on throngs of fans and followers, but when they are without their meticulous entourage of assistants, bodyguards, and screens, they often try the incognito approach to a morning coffee from Starbucks or a quick trip into Whole Foods for some organic flaxseed. Though not formally studied until this century, celebrity worship is as old as humanity. Even remote cultures have rituals for promoting those who outrank the common man. And just like the Oakley shades an American movie star may hide behind, most societies also have a way of protecting the elite from being mobbed by those who worship their lifestyle and are enamored with their fame.

The plight of stardom might be the closest connection we can make to the tricky nature of living, breathing, untarnished holiness dwelling among people like us. The Ark of the Covenant would house God's presence while He dwelled among the Israelites, but Exodus 26 shows us just how many pair of sunglasses God required to shield His glory.

In the same way that hosts of everyday Americans crowd out a celebrity spotted in a public place, the tired, wondering, wandering Hebrews would have likely steamrolled the Ark of the Covenant for a chance to experience God for themselves. Hungry for His promises to be fulfilled, they might have made a rug out of Moses on their way to the Mercy Seat were it not for the conspicuous décor and accompanying warnings not to trespass.

Was this rude on God's part? Was He being snobby or standoffish? Where is the personal heart of love buried under all those curtains?

Something tells me that God was just as anxious to get out from behind the veil as the Israelites were to hear from Him. God's style, after all, is personal connection with His creation. Sealing His holiness under plexiglass was temporary, He may have had to remind Himself, even as He ached to hold His people to His chest.

If you've experienced a life-threatening illness and have all but knocked on death's door, then you've likely seen how hospitals safeguard the air that the infirmed breathe in while recovering from transplants and the like. At first, few people can even approach their bedside, and those who do must be suited up and covered like astronauts. Sometimes there's even an air tent over the hospital bed to keep out even the tiniest pollutant in the air.

This is how Holiness was confined before Christ's death on the cross declared us pure oxygen, so to speak. It mattered little how much God wanted to walk with His people and share a meal with them and rock their babies and help them build their homes, the dilemma of Holiness—the essence of Who God is—is that it simply cannot admit any impurity. So God developed a best-case-scenario plan so that He could still be with His loves.

And, I might add, so they could feel Him.

The Nation of Israel: Key Concepts
Read Exodus 26 as you identify these key concepts.

1. Read Exodus 26:33. What was the purpose of the veil?
2. Read Exodus 26:34. Where would the mercy seat sit?
3. Where would the table for the Bread of the Presence sit? (Exodus 26:35)

_____

_____

_____

_____

_____

_____

_____

_____

_____

Thinking it through . . .

1. Without worrying about your artistic ability or lack thereof, sketch the tabernacle as best you can in the space below. If possible, use colored pencils!
2. Your sketch probably shows that the Most Holy Place is the most interior place of the tabernacle. What is the significance of this?
3. What do you think the difference was between the Holy Place and the Most Holy Place?

_____

_____

_____

_____

_____

_____

_____

_____

_____

The Church: Key Concepts

1. Read Matthew 27:51 again. To what part of the tabernacle/temple did Jesus' death on the cross give His children access, figuratively speaking?
2. Read 2 Corinthians 6:16. Where does God dwell now?
3. Read 2 Corinthians 7:1 and Hebrews 12:14. How do we keep a holy place in our temple?

_____

_____

_____

_____

_____

_____

_____

_____

_____

_____

_____

_____

_____

_____

_____

_____

_____

Thinking it through . . .

1. What does the word *holiness* mean to you? Why do you think that we tend to use that word only in church settings?

2. What is your role in sustaining your holiness? In other words, what steps do you need to take to keep yourself holy?

3. In the stormy mayhem of life, is your focus on your problems or keeping a pure heart? Keeping a realistic understanding of your own exodus, what does a proper focus look like in your situation?

_____

_____

_____

_____

_____

_____

_____

_____

LIFE LESSON 27
He never sleeps.

Have you ever had any of those "trick candles" on your birthday cake? You know the ones I'm talking about—the kind that can't be blown out, the ones that suggest, ha ha ha, that you're too old and don't have enough air left in you to blow out a small bonfire.

A fixture on the campus where I earned my undergraduate degree reminded me of these wax-covered nuisances. Erected in front of the building where commencement ceremonies were held, the "eternal flame" blazed perpetually atop an otherwise insignificant fountain. Morning, noon, and night, the flame burned. Torrential rain, occasional snow, suffocating humidity—none of these could squelch the flame. Sometimes it burned gracefully upward with the sensual curvature we ascribe to romantic illumination. Other times, it shook wildly, spitting bursts of fire out from its center haphazardly, fighting a herculean battle with rain or wind.

During the four years I lived there, that flame transitioned from a being source of intellectual curiosity for me to igniting epic inspiration for life's hardest times. I never walked by it on campus without being amazed at the tenacity of that flame.

As God wraps up the lengthy instruction manual for the tabernacle, He makes specifications for the lamp. This is a beautiful moment! Insisting on the purest of oils, God says the lamp must *stay lit at all times* as "a statute forever" (verse 21). He commands the lamp to be placed right in front of the veil that shields the Ark of the Covenant; in other words, the lamp that would burn 24 hours a day would be centered in front of the presence of God. Forgive the Vegas imagery, but I picture this as a bright neon sign in the window of God's shop that says "OPEN." All. The. Time.

King David was so pumped about this truth of God that he wrote a song about it. Psalm 121:3 sings, ". . . he who keeps you will not slumber," and—in case you missed it—verse 4 sings it again: "Behold, he who keeps Israel will neither slumber nor sleep." The prophet Isaiah would later work with God to reiterate this: "Have you not known? Have you not heard? . . . He does not faint or grow weary" (40:28).

As God established His permanent presence among His people, His loud message was that He is awake and open for business at any moment of any day. We are just as helpless as the descendants of Abraham were, so God doesn't risk any shuteye fathering us, either.

Does God sometimes feel absent from your life? Are there days when you're sure He's taking a nap on your great big pile of laundry? Rest assured, fellow traveler, that He's wide awake. His light is on, and He's anxious to warm you with His presence.

The Nation of Israel: Key Concepts

Read Exodus 27 as you identify these key concepts.

1. Read Exodus 27:1. Approximately how large was the altar?

2. Read Exodus 27:20. What word is used in your translation to describe when the lamp is to be set up?

3. Read Exodus 27:21. What is the description in this verse for when the lamp is to be tended?

_____

_____

_____

_____

_____

_____

_____

_____

Thinking it through . . .

1. What was practical about the size and other specifications of the altar?

2. Why do you think God didn't just supernaturally keep the lamp burning? In other words, why do you think He required it to be tended at all times?

3. Why do you think God required that the oils be provided by the people?

_____

_____

_____

_____

_____

_____

_____

_____

The Church: Key Concepts

1. Read Luke 23:44-46. What happens to Jesus here? What happens in the temple?
2. Read Luke 11:33. What illogical idea does Jesus point out about light?
3. Read John 8:12. What name does Jesus give Himself here? What is the promise He gives to those who walk with Him?

_____

_____

_____

_____

_____

_____

_____

_____

_____

_____

_____

_____

_____

_____

_____

Thinking it through . . .

1. Connect the size of the ancient altar of sacrifice to Jesus' ultimate sacrifice on the cross. What does that tell us about the cost of being in God's presence?

2. What does the lamp/light concept mean to you in your life?

3. What is your comfort level with the truth that God never sleeps?

_____

_____

_____

_____

_____

_____

_____

_____

God Will Finish His Work in You

(EXODUS 28-31)

LIFE LESSON 28

God's judgment of your sin is not optional . . .

If you have a teenager, you know the tremendous talent most teens have for negotiating. They know right from wrong, and they often try to leverage a lot of right as moral compensation for something wrong they've done. They are late for curfew, but they insist that they are late because they stopped to help a friend at a gas station. Or they receive a detention at school, but they swear that they respect their teacher and always obey the rules. As a parent, you know the awkward feeling that leaves you with: how to (or if to) correct a moral wrong when it appears that your child may have a redeeming explanation.

I think that nagging feeling we get inside might be the prick of our conscience, a little nudge that whispers, *"But this is still wrong."* Deep down, most of us know that wrong must be punished. Wrong is wrong, even when it is fashionably clothed in meaningful excuses.

That's easier to grasp when our children are in the wrong. But what about when it's us? Several years ago, I was driving the kids to school when we saw a police officer standing beside a car he had obviously just pulled over for speeding. Like most boys, they liked the flashing lights and the siren they heard, so I used this as a chance to show them a real-life example of breaking a rule and then having to accept the punishment for it. They listened intently as I explained speeding and its consequences.

No more than five minutes later—I promise I'm not making this up—a blue light swirled in my rearview mirror and a loud siren whirred once, commanding me to pull over. My mouth fell agape, and as my eyes dropped to my speedometer, I felt my cheeks flush with embarrassment over the Pharisee in me.

"Uh, Mommy?" Drew said gently. Jack, on the other hand, got right to the point: "There's a cop behind you!" Sure enough, I had been speeding, right as I was pointing my nicely manicured finger at another unlucky driver. In front of my kids, I knew I had to own it or else teach them that it's okay to try to wriggle out of punishment. The officer came up to my window, asked me if I knew why I had been pulled over, and listened with surprise as I said, "Yes, I was speeding. I want to thank you for pulling me over because I was just telling my boys how important it is to follow rules and laws."

Inside, I was hoping the officer would be so impressed with my humility that she wouldn't give me a ticket, but I guess she wanted to do her part to help show two young boys what happens when you break a law. She wrote me a ticket, and my boys still remind me of this irony, years after the fact.

Exodus 28 describes the ornate, elaborate priestly garment that Aaron was to wear both "for glory and for beauty" (2). God wanted him set apart, for his role as the mediator between God and His people was sacred. Despite an impressive costume and a holy calling, however, Aaron's job was ominous. Exodus 28:30 tells us, "Thus Aaron shall bear the judgment of the people of Israel on his heart before the LORD regularly."

This is like driving on the interstate with a cluster of people in a hurry and being the token car pulled over for speeding. It's like being the only one among a group of rowdy students in a classroom who is cornered in the principal's office. Aaron was to bring all the sins of all the people before the Lord—not just once, but "regularly." Ouch.

Your exodus from the bondage of addiction, sin, abuse, or another dark season does not exempt you from judgment. No matter how pitiful your situation is or how much of a victim you are, you must understand this paramount truth: God is a holy God, and He must punish sin.

You'll thank Him for it later.

The Nation of Israel: Key Concepts
Read Exodus 28 as you identify these key concepts.

1. Read Exodus 28:2-3. Why was Aaron to wear these garments, and how did God prepare the people who would make them?

2. Read verse 12 and verse 29. Why must Aaron take the names of the sons of Israel before the Lord?

3. Read verse 30. Where on his body was Aaron supposed to carry a visual representation of the judgment of Israel?

4. Read verses 34-35. What did Aaron have to wear to announce his presence as he went in the Holy Place and as he came out? What would happen if he didn't do this?

_____

_____

_____

_____

Thinking it through . . .

1. What comfort do you find in seeing God equip people for important work (verse 3)? Do you think God only equips people who choose full-time ministry as their vocation?

2. God is omnipotent and certainly not forgetful. Why do you think He wanted to be reminded regularly of His own people?

3. What part of the body did God connect to sin and judgment?

4. Why do you think God commanded Aaron to wear a bell in and out of the Holy Place?

_____

_____

_____

_____

_____

_____

_____

The Church: Key Concepts

1. Read Matthew 3:4. What was the attire of the man appointed to prepare the nation for Jesus Christ?

2. Read Proverbs 28:13. What are we encouraged to do with our sins?

3. Read Hebrews 2:2-3. What has been done for every sin?

4. Read Galatians 6:7-8. What warning does Scripture give us about maintaining a lifestyle of sin?

5. Read 1 John 1:9. What is God's promise to us when we confess our sins?

_____

_____

_____

_____

_____

_____

_____

_____

_____

_____

_____

_____

_____

_____

_____

Thinking it through . . .

1. Contrast the opulence of the Old Testament priesthood with John the Baptist's wardrobe. Why do you think they are so vastly different?

2. Do you make a conscious habit to confess your sins to God? Why or why not?

3. Is there habitual sin in your life that you need to confess right now? Look closely at your heart, and ask the Holy Spirit to show you hidden sins.

4. Do you take God's grace for granted? Are there sins you lazily commit, counting on the forgiveness you'll request later? Revisit our verses from Galatians. What does it mean to mock God?

LIFE LESSON 29

. . . because He couldn't bear to be apart from you.

In our study of Exodus 28, we explored the painful subject of the non-negotiable judgment of God. Personally, I know my podiatrist can buy another Corvette to add to his collection because the subject of sin steps on all of my toes and crushes them, leaving me limping around hopelessly. Oh, how I long to be like Jesus! Yet I am so painfully human and wretched.

Exodus 29 makes me smile, even chuckle a bit. As an avid reader, I tend to visualize scenes I come across in print and imagine how they played out in real life. With all the intricate specifications for blood, body parts, and so on, the consecration of priests must have been a little unnerving for the elders of Israel.

"Pssst!" an elder may have whispered to another. *"The kidneys are supposed to go on top of the altar, not outside! Get it right!"* As the anxious elder corrects his mistake, his accuser looks down again at the directions he's reading off of parchment. *"For the love of Pete,"* he hisses again. *"That blood was supposed to be splashed on the sides of the altar, not poured below!"*

Though I don't know how, they apparently managed to get it right eventually, and the end result was the living, breathing presence of God among them. Holiness couldn't be bought in a checkout line at their neighborhood Walmart, though; there were strict directions for creating space for a holy God to dwell among sinful people. Once they followed His guidelines, however, they could realize the loving heart of their Creator Who was desperate to be with them.

Perhaps you've just assumed that God was present in the lives of the Israelites just because . . . well, just because He was. Maybe you've never stopped to ponder *why* He insisted on living among them. I know that I had never really thought much about it until I noticed a tiny subordinate clause in verse 46. Scripture tells us here that God led them on their exodus *so that* He could live with them. He wanted to pull them out of bondage *so that* He could embrace them.

This means He was not barking out commandments just because people were getting rowdy. He was not giving cryptic directions *ad nauseum* because He was recruiting for the Mensa society. And He wasn't stomping on a nomadic, nascent people to boost His ego as SuperGod. The reason for it all—the exodus, the commandments, the laws, the sacrificial rites, and so on—the reason for *all of it* was this: He loved them, and He couldn't bear to not be with them.

So, fellow traveler, when you accept His judgment for your sin, you can expect a tsunami of love in its wake because *He can't bear to be without you.*

The Nation of Israel: Key Concepts

Read Exodus 29 as you identify these key concepts.

1. Read Exodus 29:4 and 20. What two fluids had to be on the priests to make them holy before the Lord?

2. Read Exodus 29:42. What does God say He will do as the priests regularly offer burnt offerings?

3. Read Exodus 29:43-44. How does God make it possible for sinful people to be in His presence?

4. Read Exodus 29:45. What is the end result of all these preparations?

_____

_____

_____

_____

_____

_____

_____

_____

_____

Thinking it through . . .

1. As you read through the first 40+ verses of Exodus 29, did the consecration process seem logical or random to you? What was your reaction to the process?

2. What significance do you see in the use of water and blood to prepare the priests?

3. Write out verses 45-46 in your own words—everyday common language. Now read what you wrote. What do you imagine it felt like for everyday people to hear that God wanted to dwell among them?

_____

_____

_____

_____

_____

_____

_____

_____

_____

The Church: Key Concepts

1. Read Matthew 28:19. How were the apostles supposed to make disciples out of people?

2. Read 1 Peter 3:21-22. How are we consecrated for God?

3. Read 1 Peter 2:9. Who are God's priests now? (Note how God calls you out of darkness as you continue your exodus!)

4. Read Galatians 3:27. What garment, so to speak, did we put on in baptism?

5. Read Galatians 4:6. Where did God send His Spirit for you?

_____

_____

_____

_____

_____

_____

_____

_____

_____

_____

_____

_____

_____

_____

_____

_____

Thinking it through . . .

1. How are you now set apart for God through water and blood, like the Old Testament priests were?

2. What do you know about the work of a priest? Is it difficult to picture yourself in that role?

3. Why do you think God made us His priesthood, instead of leaving a "middle man" between Him and us?

_____

_____

_____

_____

_____

_____

_____

_____

LIFE LESSON 30
Your gifts to the Lord are precious to Him.

I am privileged to own a rare piece of pottery. Both beautiful and practical, I use it to store my cleaning cloths. It's a square box, and the rich, leathery brown glaze is accented with splashes of regal purple. I love purple! There are window-like holes around its perimeter, and this adds to the uniqueness. Every time I reach for a cleaning cloth (which, I admit, isn't as often as it needs to be), I feel a hug around my heart as I touch such a precious gift.

Though I am sure I have carnal tendencies buried somewhere, I don't think of myself as materialistic. I prefer simple over extravagant, casual over fancy, less instead of more. My husband gets nervous, in fact, whenever I start gearing up to hold a garage sale. I can't stand clutter, and he jokes that I would put a price tag on him if he stood still long enough! Other than our family scrapbooks, there are few inanimate objects in our home with which I couldn't part.

This piece of pottery, however, is an exception. I wouldn't take even the highest bid for it. I would never, ever sell it! It is absolutely sacred to me.

I should probably tell you that this piece of pottery was shaped by the soft, eight-year-old hands of my son, Jack. The sides kind of fall in toward the center, as if it's contemplating being a teepee. The top rim is a bit jagged, and the colors appear in random intensity over the piece—some places are heavy and dark, while others show only a light, haphazard brushstroke. The "windows" are strangely oriented polygons. My favorite part of the whole box, though, is the bottom of it, where the letters J – A – C – K are etched in elementary handwriting.

You wouldn't offer me fifty cents for this dilapidated ceramic container, yet it is one of my most cherished treasures. I'm sure you know why. Sweet Jack made it just for his mommy, and no original masterpiece anywhere in the world is worth more in my eyes.

Has it ever occurred to you that God holds dear the gifts that you give Him? In the same way a teacher cherishes a handmade Valentine from a darling kindergartener, God cherishes the gifts you offer Him out of love. Exodus 30 describes the offerings that the Israelites would bring before the Lord. Certainly, these gifts were to be unique, uncommon, and preciously prepared. But God wasn't trying to check off items from His vast gift registry; He cherished these offerings. They were "most holy to the LORD" (verse 10).

You may not have much to give back to God as you continue your exodus, but rest assured that your gift of love makes the U.S. Mint look like a gumball machine. So grab your glue and popsicle sticks and shamelessly offer God the best you have.

The Nation of Israel: Key Concepts

Read Exodus 30 as you identify these key concepts.

1. Read Exodus 30:8. How often were the people to offer incense?

2. Read Exodus 30:10. What was "most holy to the Lord"?

3. Read Exodus 30:14-15. What were the directions for the rich? For the poor?

4. Read Exodus 30:37-38. How would the offering to the Lord be special?

_____

_____

_____

_____

_____

_____

_____

_____

_____

Thinking it through . . .

1. Why do you think there were so many types of offerings and so many specific directions for them?

2. Why do you think the rich and the poor were to give the same offering for atonement?

3. Why do you think God had to tell the people that His gifts were to be pricey, sacred, and not mundane?

_____

_____

_____

_____

_____

_____

_____

_____

The Church: Key Concepts

1. Read 1 Chronicles 21:24. What was King David's mindset toward gifts offered to God?

2. Read 2 Corinthians 9:6-7. What principles of giving does the Apostle Paul lay out for Christians?

3. Read Luke 21:1-4. Why is the widow's gift more valuable than the rich man's?

_____

_____

_____

_____

_____

_____

_____

_____

_____

_____

_____

_____

_____

_____

_____

Thinking it through . . .

1. What are some examples of gifts that we give to God?

2. Do we tend to give God our leftovers, or do we make intentional sacrifices to give to Him? Why is this?

3. What gift do you offer regularly to God? What can you give Him that is out of your comfort zone?

4. Have you ever been ashamed or embarrassed to give to God? Or, conversely, do you have a tendency to give with a proud, showy heart?

_____

_____

_____

_____

_____

_____

_____

_____

LIFE LESSON 31
God has equipped you for His work.

Before Netflix, before DVR, before the Internet made watching a favorite movie possible at any time of any day, *The Wizard of Oz* used to be televised around March every year. You may remember, like I do, seeing it listed in the TV Guide and sitting down right at 8:00 p.m. to the black-and-white Kansas scene and having to will your bladder to hold until the next commercial.

You know the story. Dorothy and her three unlikely friends set out in pursuit of a great wizard they've never met to beg for things they think they need but later realize they already possess. Dorothy, ironically, thinks she needs to travel far away to figure out how to get back home. The tin man—so compassionate that it's a wonder he doesn't die of tetanus—thinks he needs a heart, and the scarecrow assumes he needs a brain simply because he lacks a sense of direction. And the lion—don't we all love the lion? In comparing himself to other lions, he overlooks the oddity that he's the only biped among them, but he's quite sure that he needs a dose of courage to make him more like his similarly maned peers.

Since we know how the story ends, let's jump straight to the obvious lesson here: Each character goes on a long, unnecessary search for something already within them. Is it because their own gifts don't look the way they think they should? Perhaps because their own weaknesses intimidate them? Regardless of the reason, each traveler feels inadequate.

Maybe we like the music. Maybe we like the munchkins. Maybe we have a neighbor we wouldn't mind dousing with water. I venture to say, however, that one additional reason we watch *The Wizard of Oz* is that something in all of us bears witness to the feeling of *just not being good enough.*

In the lavish detail and seeming superfluity of the ark of the covenant, the tabernacle, the priestly garments, and the offerings, God was ten steps ahead of Moses in preparing people ahead of time who had the talent to make these items according to God's specifications. "I have given to all able men ability, that they may make all that I have commanded you," God assures Moses in Exodus 31:6. Imagine Moses's slightly raised eyebrows, then, as God then explains that Moses will "speak to the people of Israel" (verse 12).

Lord, I thought we'd covered this. I don't speak well, remember? Moses may have prayed. How kind of God to equip the craftsmen to do their work, so can't He find someone with a degree in public speaking to bring yet another message to the people? By this time, though, Moses doesn't seem to argue with God. He knows he's not going to get out of this one.

Maybe he's also learned something about God—i.e., that He doesn't equip us based on standard job requirements. He gives us what we need to do His work, though our qualifications may not appear to be adequate in our own eyes.

Cancel your trip to Oz. Embrace the opportunities before you. You were created to do His good works, so click your heels together, and get started!

The Nation of Israel: Key Concepts

Read Exodus 31 as you identify these key concepts.

1. With what unique skills did God gift Bezalel? (Exodus 31:3-5)
2. What items would other skilled craftsmen make? (Exodus 31:6-11)
3. Who wrote the message God had for His people? (Exodus 31:18)

_____

_____

_____

_____

_____

_____

_____

_____

Thinking it through . . .

1. Do you think these craftsmen knew they were destined to build something for God?
2. Which came first—their being equipped or their having the opportunity to serve?
3. Why do you think God wrote the message in stone with His own finger? Couldn't He have appointed a mason to inscribe His message?

_____

_____

_____

_____

_____

_____

_____

_____

_____

The Church: Key Concepts

1. According to Ephesians 2:10, who are you and why were you created?

2. Read 1 Corinthians 12:4-11. What does Paul tell the Corinthians about spiritual gifts?

3. Who gives power and equips them all? (1 Corinthians 12:6)

4. What are some of the apostolic gifts Paul uses as examples of the diversity in the body of Christ? (See 1 Corinthians 12:8-10)

5. How does God portion out gifts and abilities? (1 Corinthians 12:11)

_____

_____

_____

_____

_____

_____

_____

_____

_____

_____

_____

_____

_____

_____

_____

_____

Thinking it through . . .

1. What are some talents, skills, and gifts that you have?

2. Have you turned down opportunities to serve God and bless others? Why?

3. Is it possible that you have gifts of which you're unaware? Do you think God will only call you to do things that you feel confident doing? Explain.

_____

_____

_____

_____

_____

_____

_____

_____

God Leaves No Stone Unturned

(EXODUS 32-34)

LIFE LESSON 32

You don't need a cow.

So much of our faith in God seems fickle, prone to ebb and flow based on how closely God adheres to the timeline we've set for Him. We pray for a miracle, some deliverance, a specific financial provision, or even for a companion with whom to share this season of life. When our patience runs low or our panic sets in, however, we assume that God needs some assistance. We made Him an appointment, but He's a no show.

Is there anything I can do for you? I mean, I'm praying, but what can I do to help? your sweet, well-intentioned sisters in Christ ask you. Even they seem a bit antsy that God's taking His time, as if—perhaps this time—God wants to just watch you fix your own issues.

Maybe God isn't giving you a baby on your schedule, so you rush into expensive medical intervention despite your husband's complaints. Maybe your teenage daughter is longing to fit in at school; you've been praying for her, but she seems to be needier every day. You give in and allow her to wear an immodest outfit, hoping to soothe her. Or perhaps you're praying for relief from debt. Your attention span for prayer and budgeting makes a house fly seem lethargic, so you buy a handful of lottery tickets hoping for a windfall to whisk away your student loans and credit card bills.

We are most prone to idolatry when we are uncomfortable, so embracing the transforming power of pain and the gracious rest in limbo is a critical turn to take in our exodus. If it's any consolation, the Israelites were no more patient than we are when waiting on God. Moses had ascended Sinai to have a powwow with God, and he'd been gone for a long time. In fact, for all they knew, he could have dropped off the grid completely . . . after all, the guy seemed too old for this kind of hike anyway. His cellphone is going straight to voicemail, and he's not answering his texts.

He's not coming back, one hungry Hebrew says as he looks back up the mountain. *He was probably on the lunch menu for the mountain lions last week, and here we are still expecting him to walk on down.* Other men see the likelihood and agree. *We can't keep going without a god, though,* another reminds them as he chews mindlessly on a leather strap he's twiddling. *Aaron! Let's go to Aaron!* and they all stand simultaneously to begin their trek toward Aaron's tent.

As you've probably heard, the end result is a 14-karat cow. And an angry, angry God.

The Nation of Israel: Key Concepts

Read Exodus 32 as you identify these key concepts.

1. Read Exodus 32:1. Why did the people lose hope in Moses?

2. Read Exodus 32:3-6. What items did Aaron build? What was the response of the Israelites?

3. Why did God want to be left alone after this? (Exodus 32:10)

4. Moses convinces God to change His mind about destroying them (Exodus 32:14), but does God still punish them for this blatant idolatry? With what? (Exodus 32:35)

_____

_____

_____

_____

_____

_____

_____

_____

Thinking it through . . .

1. For what were the Israelites longing? Whose idea was the cow?

2. Why do you think Aaron, of all people, caved?

3. What are all the reasons that God is angry?

4. Speculate about the nature of the punishment plague. What do you think the Israelites may have experienced during this discipline?

_____

_____

_____

_____

_____

_____

_____

_____

_____

The Church: Key Concepts

1. Read Romans 8:25. How are we to wait?

2. Read Romans 5:6. When did Christ die? What does this tell us about God's timing?

3. Read Galatians 5:19-21. Is idolatry warned against in the New Testament church?

4. Read 1 John 5:20-21. What is true about God? What plea does John make as he ends this letter?

_____

_____

_____

_____

_____

_____

_____

_____

_____

_____

_____

_____

_____

_____

_____

_____

Thinking it through . . .

1. When you're praying about something, do you struggle with patience in waiting on God's answer?

2. What types of things do you do when your prayers don't seem to be getting the answers you want?

3. Read Isaiah 44:9-20, where Isaiah describes the nature of idolatry. What kinds of things have become idols in our lives? Think especially about things to which you turn that make you more comfortable, things that make "waiting" easier, or things to which you turn when you're feeling uptight.

4. If you have time, do a quick online search for the number of times idolatry is mentioned in Scripture. What does this tell you about how prone you are to turn to idols instead of God?

_____

_____

_____

_____

_____

_____

_____

_____

_____

LIFE LESSON 33
God is protecting you.

Of all forty chapters in the book, Exodus 33 might be the most revealing of the parental instincts of God. Still brooding over the golden rib eye, He is mad as a hornet and needs a mental health day. He appoints an angel to babysit so He can cool down, but, doggone it, it's hard to stay angry when the pure, pleading heart of Moses is standing in front of Him.

Like an innocent three-year-old who has a long history of being loved like crazy, Moses presumes the evanescence of God's anger and jumps right into myriad requests for God's help. He has God wrapped around his arthritic finger, and God melts into Moses's pleas. Handing over His credit card, God says *yes* to going with Moses and his ragtag bunch, yes to restoration and mercy, and, not surprisingly, *yes* to revealing Himself yet again.

What a ball of mush! The chapter opens with God mad enough to ignite a snowball, but within a handful of verses He's hovering over Moses like a father over his tiny newborn child. Though the calf is still a touchy subject, God forgets that He's booked a one-way ticket to Anywhere-But-Here, and is soon doing a drive-by so that Moses can be extra sure of Him.

How completely and utterly like a parent! We can be so irate at our children over their disobedience, negligence, disrespect—you name it! But, without a thought, we can turn on a dime the second our child calls for help or crawls up on our lap with a sticky-fingered hug. We long to please them, to see them happy, but we all know that sometimes protecting our children means they might have to be uncomfortable for a little bit.

Living in the South, we are ever watchful during late summer months for tornadoes. About two years ago, our town's sirens went off early one morning, just before we were about to get up to begin the work day. Irritated at my last few minutes of sleep being interrupted, I pulled my covers up a little higher and hoped the sirens would go off as quickly as they had begun. My husband, however, was already in the boys' room hoisting Jack off the top bunk and barking at Drew to wake up and move quickly to the shelter. Reluctantly, I got up, grabbed the cat, and followed Steve and the kids out to the dark, damp crypt-like space built into the ground behind our house. All in the name of safety and protection, my husband commandeered us to a black, creepy place (where spiders and snakes have occasionally held morning worship). Twenty minutes later, we emerged unharmed by the passing winds.

We were made in the image of God (Genesis 1:26), so don't think for one minute that any of us wrote the book on parenting. Every instinct to love, to protect, to nurture, and to shelter our children is the mirror image of the parenting heart of God.

Look around you. If all you can see is darkness, you might just be tucked so far into His chest that Satan can't even tell that God is hiding you "until the storms of destruction pass by" (Psalm 57:1).

The Nation of Israel: Key Concepts

Read Exodus 33 as you identify these key concepts.

1. How do Exodus 33:1-3 show both the love of God and the anger of God toward the children of Israel?

2. Read Exodus 33:11. How did the Lord used to speak to Moses?

3. Read Exodus 33:15 and then back up to verse 14. What does Moses not want to travel without? What is God's promise?

4. Read Exodus 33:18. What is Moses's request?

5. Read Exodus 33:21-23. Where will Moses be while God's glory passes by?

_____

_____

_____

_____

_____

_____

_____

_____

Thinking it through . . .

1. Do you see Moses twisting God's arm (heart) in this chapter, in much the same way a child begs a parent for support? What does that tell you about his relationship with God?

2. Do you feel a special intimacy with God, "as a man speaks to his friend" (v. 11)?

3. God had promised to send an angel with the Israelites, but why do you think Moses seems to press God for His presence?

4. Moses had seen a lot of miracles! Why, then, do you think he asks God to show him His glory?

5. Think about the lighting conditions (or lack thereof) in a rock's cleft. What emotions might Moses have felt while curled up in the cleft of the rock? What was happening during this darkness?

_____

_____

_____

_____

_____

_____

_____

_____

The Church: Key Concepts

1. Read Psalm 57:1 and Psalm 91:4. Where does the psalmist envision God hiding us during hard times? What would the lighting conditions be here?

2. Read Psalm 30:5 and 103:8. Does God have a quick temper? How long does God's anger last?

3. Read Hebrews 13:5-8. What truths of God, His character, and His love for you are revealed in these verses?

4. Read 2 Corinthians 4:7. Where is the treasure of the life-changing gospel stored, figuratively speaking? What would these lighting conditions be?

5. Read verses 8-10. Describe the protection we have in Jesus Christ.

_____

_____

_____

_____

_____

_____

_____

_____

_____

_____

_____

_____

_____

_____

_____

_____

_____

Thinking it through . . .

1. Can you think of a dark season of life or a particular difficult experience you've had that, looking back, reveals God's protection of you?

2. What are your thoughts about the anger of God? How does this compare or contrast with the parenting styles with which you are familiar?

3. Do you have an awareness of God's constant, hovering presence, love, and protection over you?

4. If you have time, search online for the protective properties of clay/pottery. What new understanding does this give you for 2 Corinthians 4:7?

5. Describe the season of life you are currently in. Is it dark, or is this a calm, joyous time? What are you learning about God that you can apply to this time in your journey?

_____

_____

_____

_____

_____

_____

_____

_____

_____

LIFE LESSON 34
This is your God!

Santa Claus is not on my nice list. Although I love his bright red, fur-trimmed wardrobe and share his affinity for snow and mammals, I struggle to appreciate anyone or anything who attempts to share glory with God. If we decide to celebrate the birth of Christ in December, we probably shouldn't allow Santa Claus to crash the party. If we decide, however, to celebrate the holiday season as simply a culturally-based time of giving, mirth, and celebration, then, by all means, send an invitation to the North Pole.

An equally nagging reason I'm not a fan of the jolly old man with the toys, though, seeps into the carnal nature I wish I could shed once and for all. You see, Santa's mass appeal seems to be in *what we can get* from him. Children sit on his lap and beg for ponies, Legos, and burping baby dolls. No one is interested in his character, and most don't even care if his beard is fake because we are enamored with an opportunity to make a wish list and be so bold as to say what we want to see under the tree with our name on it. As a Christmas baby, I have an embarrassing track record of doubly lengthy lists and grand expectations of what I will *get*.

I'm worried that we are the same way with God. We arrive on two wheels to church, barely in time for Bible class, and we carry in a lengthy list of prayer requests. And, because His heart is bigger than Texas, God welcomes and tends to every single request we have, both voiced and unspoken. If we aren't careful, though, we might end up relating to God much like we relate to Santa Claus. We might value God for *what we can get* and miss the sheer magnificence of Who He is. As a result, our faith falters because we're basing it on a list that still has a few requests on backorder.

When we worship God for Who He is, though, and meditate on the truths of His character, our faith needs no more caffeine to stay alive and vibrant with hope. As Moses and God meet up again—incidentally, after both of them have chilled out a little—God reminds Moses of Who He is. In the wake of Israel's affair with the cow, God makes His flawless character abundantly clear. He is love. He is faithful. He is good. But He's no doormat. He is jealous, and He will punish unfaithfulness.

As you journey with God, you must know Who He is. Invest prayer and Bible reading time in learning the character of God. You will find yourself celebrating Him all year long.

The Nation of Israel: Key Concepts

Read Exodus 34 as you identify these key concepts.

1. Read Exodus 34:1 again. What is God helping Moses to remake?

2. Read Exodus 34:6 and 7. Copy those verses below, circling characteristics of God.

3. Read Exodus 34:14. What does God say His name is?

4. Read Exodus 34:28. What was the end result of Moses's time with God?

5. Read Exodus 34:29. What was unique about Moses's appearance after he had been with God?

_____

_____

_____

_____

_____

_____

_____

_____

_____

Thinking it through . . .

1. What does it say about God's character that He invests in remaking the stone tablets and renewing the covenant that had been violated by the Israelites?

2. Which seems bigger—God's determination to love and show His faithfulness or His commitment to judging and punishing wrongdoing? Explain.

3. Compare the worship of the golden calf to an extramarital affair. What is God jealous about?

4. Why do you think God lit up Moses's face after meetings with Him?

_____

_____

_____

_____

_____

_____

_____

_____

_____

The Church: Key Concepts

1. Read Luke 4:18-19. In what way was Jesus' mission similar to God's renewing His covenant with Israel?

2. Read 1 John 4:7-8. Fill in the blank: God is _____. Now read 1 Corinthians 13:4-7, substituting "God" each time you see the word *love*. What does this tell you about God's character?

3. Read Psalm 34:5. What is characteristic of those who stay focused on God?

_____

_____

_____

_____

_____

_____

_____

_____

_____

_____

_____

_____

_____

_____

_____

Thinking it through . . .

1. Does it warm your heart that God reconciled with Israel after they had betrayed Him so overtly? What does that tell you about the way God will behave toward you when you fail Him?

2. Which aspects of God's character are hardest for you to believe in and cherish as true?

3. Do you think people who trust God have a visibly different look about them? Have you ever witnessed someone with a radiant appearance?

4. What can you do to focus your faith more on God's character, rather than on the way He answers your prayers?

_____

_____

_____

_____

_____

_____

_____

_____

⟿ SESSION 11 ⟿

God Leaves Nothing to Be Desired

(EXODUS 35-36)

LIFE LESSON 35

Be a giver.

McDonald's is probably one of few entities that actually manages to start and finish a game of Monopoly within the lifespan of a hamburger. Most of us start the game and quit somewhere around St. Charles Place. In fact, as a typical mother who is plagued by exhaustion and endless to-do lists, I think the most depressing request from my children on family game night is Monopoly. The game is interminable, and after three hours of getting out of jail free, I'm ready to quit and claim everything I own—both in the game and in real life—just to declare myself the official loser and end the game.

So, yes. I hate Monopoly.

McDonald's Monopoly, however, is playable. For those of us who have finite attention spans, we are relieved that the game starts and ends on specific dates. Well, heck, it actually *ends* at all. We might win a free cheeseburger at a railroad crossing, and we have incentive to supersize our fries so that we can get additional game pieces. McDonald's Monopoly is fun!

The story goes that, thirty-some years ago, someone won the coveted Park Place and Boardwalk pieces. Instead of coming forward to claim the million-dollar prize, however, this person taped the two pieces to a blank sheet of paper and placed them in an unmarked envelope. Then, he or she mailed them with no return address to St. Jude's Children's Research Hospital, a nonprofit intensive care facility in Memphis, Tennessee that charges patients nothing for their treatment and care. If this story is true, St. Jude's may have cashed in on a 1 million dollar donation from Mr. or Mrs. Nobody.

But the donation isn't what I remember media focusing on. All the talk was about the incredible selflessness, generosity, and humility of the giver. In exchange for clogged arteries from nonperishable chicken nuggets and the best-tasting fries on the planet, this man or woman won a million-dollar prize . . . only to quietly send it away, declaring St. Jude's the winner.

Fact or fiction, this seems to be a story God would "Like" on Facebook. Giving so willingly, so humbly, so preciously melts God's heart like butter in a microwave.

The thing is . . . sometimes we become a little self-absorbed during an exodus. We're weary. We're stressed. We're ashamed. We're anxious. We are overwhelmed. Like a hyper middle school boy having to sit still in math class, the pain and discomfort of our journey cries out for us to pay attention only to ourselves. We might put some money in the plate on Sunday morning, but sometimes it's more out of habit or obligation than out of an excited, willing heart.

I heard a missionary talk about a church he once visited in an impoverished, foreign country. When it was time to give the offering, the entire congregation erupted in enthusiastic applause! They dug out whatever small amount they had and sang a song of thanksgiving as they passed the plate. The minister later shared with the awe-struck missionary that his congregation felt honored that God would want something that they had, and they were excited to give anything and everything to Him.

Drop the mic!

The Nation of Israel: Key Concepts
Read Exodus 35 as you identify these key concepts.

1. Read Exodus 35:5, 21, 22, 26, and 29. What phrase or phrases are repeated?

2. What did God desire from people who had talent with any kind of craft or skilled trade? (See Exodus 35:10 and 25.)

3. Focus on Exodus 35:25-26. What role did women play in the making of the priestly garments and the tabernacle?

_____

_____

_____

_____

_____

_____

_____

_____

Thinking it through . . .

1. Why do you think God requested contributions be made only from those who had willing hearts? Couldn't He have just commanded them to give, especially after all they had done against Him?

2. What about people who weren't talented in any of the ways that God needed for the tabernacle and priestly preparations? What if they didn't even have any jewels, wood, or yarns to bring as gifts? What do you think God desired from them?

3. Does it surprise you to see women so prominently serving in the Lord's house? Why or why not?

_____

_____

_____

_____

_____

_____

_____

_____

_____

The Church: Key Concepts

1. Read Matthew 6:2-4 and 2 Corinthians 9:7. How are we to give? What type of giver does God love?

2. Regardless of what your talents are, how should you use them? (See Colossians 3:23.)

3. Read Luke 21:1-4. What impressed Jesus about the widow?

_____

_____

_____

_____

_____

_____

_____

_____

_____

_____

_____

_____

_____

_____

_____

_____

_____

_____

Thinking it through . . .

1. Take an honest look at your heart. Do you get excited about giving to the Lord's work? Is it hard for you to give without announcing it to others for even a small amount of recognition? When is it hardest for you to give?

2. In what ways do you give your talents to the Lord? Are there talents that you have of which you need to offer God more?

3. Since you are a woman, perhaps a woman with limited financial means, does God still desire gifts from you? Why doesn't He let you off the hook with giving?

_____

_____

_____

_____

_____

_____

_____

LIFE LESSON 36

We don't get to make the rules for worship—or add to them.

Exodus 36 is one of those chapters that probably bores even the most determined reader of the Old Testament. It reads like perhaps a behind-the-scenes outline for an HGTV home remodeling series. We admire the finished product and make wish lists to transform our mundane spaces into magazine photos, but we have little patience for minutia along the way. Show producers sense our hunger for the "after," so they dramatize the "before," but filter out most of the labor in between.

Why would God inspire Moses to include in Exodus what seems like the entire assembly manual for the tabernacle? Do you and I really need to know how many loops were sewn in the curtains or the precise dimensions of the wooden tabernacle frame? Does God want us to rush to Hobby Lobby for fabric and begin working on curtains of a similar pattern? Should the men of our congregations reconsider our buildings' architectural plans and rush to a home improvement warehouse to buy supplies for God's holy woodwork?

We know that the obvious answer is *no*, that God doesn't expect us to design our worship spaces in this fashion. Though we can travel around the world and tour some of the most breathtaking, jaw-dropping cathedrals that might rival the opulence of the tabernacle, God is no more impressed with our worship from those spaces than He is from the songs we sing to Him in the shower each morning.

So why include the instruction manual? I'm not sure, but I wonder if God wanted to emphasize His supremacy in ordering our worship. Imagine what the tabernacle might have looked like if God had simply invited the Israelites to design it themselves, especially in the wake of their adulterous affair with beef. God would protect the sanctity of true, acceptable worship to Yahweh, a task too sacred to leave to the imaginations of His well-meaning but fickle followers. Could God be sending us the same message today? In this overly technical, yawn-inducing chapter, might God want us to get the message that *He lays the ground rules for worship?*

If that's true, then buried in this chapter may be His gentle reminder that He does not want our "add-ons" either. You probably know exactly what I mean here. We bake a cake from a delicious recipe we've found on Pinterest; the chocolate icing tastes great, but we decide to dust it with powdered sugar just to improve the cake's plate appeal. Or, we find directions for a salad—to be served out of Mason jars, of course—but we substitute the called-for walnuts with roasted almonds because we like the taste of them better. Ironically, our God-given creativity is the gift that enables us to make these beautiful, tasty, and pleasing substitutions and additions to our DIY projects.

But Scripture doesn't support that approach in worship. The plenteous gifts of fabric, gemstones, wood, and yarn piled up so high that Moses probably contemplated a yard sale. He tells God that they have plenty of supplies to do the work God had commanded; God's response, then, is to stop accepting gifts. In fact verse 6 says that "the people were restrained" from bringing anything else.

I can imagine a few eager servants making innocent suggestions, though. "Look, we've got all this extra wood, why don't we build a—," to which Moses probably responded with a firm palm-to-face "NO." We're not adding a single stitch more than God has ordered. We're not adding a shadow box with Moses's staff. We're not adding a fossilized frog from Egypt. We're not adding *anything*.

Where is our worship space today? Is it a building? No! Today, because the blood of Jesus Christ connected us directly to the Most Holy Place, our worship space has been remodeled to look like a human heart. But, let's remember, God still makes the rules.

This is no time for DIY-ers. We need the Master Builder.

The Nation of Israel: Key Concepts

Read Exodus 36 as you identify these key concepts.

1. Read Exodus 36:1. What did God do for Bezalel and Oholiab?

2. Read Exodus 36:2. Who else came to do the work of building the worship space?

3. Read Exodus 36:5-7. What happened? Why were the people restrained from bringing more?

Thinking it through . . .

1. How do you think the talented craftsmen were identified? What do you notice *still* about their hearts for this work?

2. Why do you think God would not accept additional materials and gifts? Couldn't they have been put to good use? Do you think people were hurt over not being allowed to bring more?

_____

_____

_____

_____

_____

_____

_____

_____

The Church: Key Concepts

1. Read John 4:24. How are we to worship God?

2. Read Hebrews 12:28. What type of worship are we to offer God?

3. Read Revelation 4:10-11. Describe this scene of heavenly worship.

_____

_____

_____

_____

_____

_____

_____

_____

_____

_____

_____

_____

_____

_____

_____

_____

Thinking it through . . .

1. What does worship look like in a congregational meeting? How can we worship God in our daily lives?

2. What are ways we have made substitutions or have added on to scriptural worship? How have we justified this?

3. Does the New Testament leave worship style and format up to us? Explain.

_____

_____

_____

_____

_____

_____

_____

_____

God Won't Leave You Hanging

(EXODUS 37-38)

LIFE LESSON 37

He offers you mercy.

The sight in front of Merilla Cuthbert is pitiful. As she sits at the foot of the bed and stares at the prostrate orphan child Anne Shirley, the stern, often icy Merilla is aghast. Anne's infamous red hair is doused with a putrid green, the result of a bad hair dye. To make matters worse, Merilla has just been informed that Anne, a precocious child sent to the Cuthberts by mistake, lost her temper at school and broke a slate over the head of Gilbert Blythe.

"You *really* broke your slate over that boy's head?" Merilla asks the forlorn Anne.

"Yes," Anne meekly answers, terrified that she has now completely ruined her chances of ever being adopted by the Cuthberts.

"Hard?"

"Very hard, I'm afraid," Anne admits honestly.

"I know I should be angry—I should be furious!" Merilla responds. "But, if you promise me that nothing of this sort will happen again, I won't say another word about it."

(*Pause the DVD and grab a Kleenex.*)

"You're not going to send me back?" Anne whispers, afraid to believe.

"I've come to a decision. The trial is over. You will remain at Green Gables."

"Merilla!" Anne gasps.

"I think you may be a kindred spirit after all," Merilla says in a rare moment of gentleness and affection. Because of that moment, Anne Shirley became the timeless classic *Anne of Green Gables*.

Christians are often guilty of thinking we are "on trial," like Anne. We feel like our adoption into the kingdom of heaven depends on our not making any mistakes, on behaving well, and doing good things that would make God proud. We know Judgment is coming, so we try to wash up and dress in our Sunday best—only to fall in the mud right as we walk out the door.

Judgment is coming, but that's what God *will do* (future tense verb). Mercy, however, is what *God is doing* (present participle verb). In other words, what sits in front of you at this moment is the tremendous mercy of God. His mercy is what gives you the right to be called a child of God, an heir to the kingdom of heaven.

You might be expecting Him to kick you out, crushing your hope of adoption into His family. After all, you're a mess. Your attempt to dye your hair, so to speak, backfired, naturally, for your attempts at righteousness are as wretched as the sanitary products a woman uses on her monthly cycles (Isaiah 64:6). You bury your head and brace yourself for His scorn.

You don't hear Him at first. You were waiting for a lecture, but you'd swear you'd just heard a gentle whisper (1 Kings 19:11-13) instead. And you're right. No need for cotton swabs; you're hearing just fine. God is indeed extending His loving, affectionate, merciful hand to you at precisely the time when you were expecting to spontaneously combust under His wrath.

God's perch among the nation of Israel was on a seat of mercy. Exodus 37 highlights the lavish nature of that mercy and the purity of God's presence on it. The ark is made of pure gold, and the two angels that hover over the mercy seat are molded from the same flawless metal. God had every right to call His place a Judgment Seat; after all, the Israelites were faltering in their faithfulness to His commands.

Instead, however, He named His chair the Mercy Seat. Though they deserved fire and damnation, He offered them grace and love, making them kindred spirits after all.

The Nation of Israel: Key Concepts

Read Exodus 37 as you identify these key concepts.

1. Read Exodus 37:6, 7, and 9. What is God's place called?
2. Read Exodus 37:7-9. What type of angel is crafted to face the Mercy Seat?
3. What other items does Bezalel build in this chapter? From what are they made?

_____

_____

_____

_____

_____

_____

_____

_____

_____

Thinking it through . . .

1. Do you think God was setting Himself up for disappointment and a broken heart by offering Himself as a Merciful Father instead of a Judge?

2. Why do you think Bezalel put angels above the Mercy Seat? Why would God have ordered this?

3. Why do you think God demanded that every single part of the tabernacle and its contents be built with this level of extravagance?

_____

_____

_____

_____

_____

_____

_____

_____

The Church: Key Concepts

1. Read James 2:13. What is the relationship between mercy and judgment?

2. Read 1 Peter 1:3 and Ephesians 2:4. How is God's mercy described?

3. Read Romans 9:14-16. What does Paul remind us about God's words to Moses?

_____

_____

_____

_____

_____

_____

_____

_____

_____

_____

_____

_____

_____

_____

_____

_____

Thinking it through . . .

1. Do you tend to view God as harsh and judgmental or affectionate and merciful?

2. What does it mean to you that "mercy triumphs over judgment"?

3. Do you think God desires to show mercy to all people, or does He withhold mercy in some situations? Search the Scriptures to help you think through this question.

_____

_____

_____

_____

_____

_____

_____

_____

LIFE LESSON 38
You have a place.

P.E. was always a nightmare for me. As some of my older loved ones in the South say, "Some's got it, some's h'ain't." Translation: Some people are gifted athletes. Some people have less athletic ability than a stale piece of bread. As a slice of that loaf, I dreaded the beginning of class when the elite athletes got to pick their teams. Thankfully, P.E. teachers today have eradicated this method of social annihilation, but the old school method of taking turns picking your players always—and I mean always—left me standing alone at the end, feeling sheepish and embarrassed.

In sharing this story, I certainly want no pity—unless it's for the captains who had to claim me. I wouldn't have picked me either! After all, I was small and slow and uncoordinated. I once got the basketball and started running toward the other team's goal, completely oblivious. Though I spent years wishing I were gifted in some way on a ball field or in a gym, I just didn't have any business being on any team's roster.

Exodus 38, however, makes me feel like the pick of the litter. It seems like God carved out a place for everybody in the important work of building His earthly dwelling place. I love how often women are mentioned in these last few chapters, for they contributed just as eagerly and significantly as the men did. I love that there were givers. There were builders. There were embroiderers. There were record keepers.

For a few chapters, I've received this vibe that *anyone whose heart was willing* would be given a job to do. What an honor! The psalmist said, "I would rather be a doorkeeper in the house of my God than dwell in the tents of wickedness" (Psalm 84:10). I hear him yearning for any spot on God's team—even if it's the water boy—because even being the lowest peon on God's team is better than showing up on any earthly A-list.

So your degree of talent for singing or preaching or teaching or comforting doesn't seem to be an issue for God. He still has a place for you to serve. You may feel like you're bound to be ousted when God makes His final cuts for kingdom service, but would it surprise you to know that you are precisely the person He is looking for? He has just the right opportunity for you! Your willing, eager heart is all He needed to pull your job off CraigsList and claim that the position has been filled.

Team Heaven includes you, so suit up!

The Nation of Israel: Key Concepts

Read Exodus 38 as you identify these key concepts.

....

1. Read Exodus 38:1. Who is the "he" mentioned here?

2. Read Exodus 38:8. Where did Bezalel get the mirrors to help make the bronze?

3. Read Exodus 38:21-23. Outline all those who were in charge of the making of the tabernacle.

_____

_____

_____

_____

_____

_____

_____

_____

Thinking it through . . .

....

1. Do you think Bezalel would have felt honored to do this work? Overwhelmed? Indifferent? How would you feel if you were in such a position?

2. What is the significance of where the women mentioned in this chapter did their ministry?

3. Can you imagine any type of person/worker that would have been turned away from the work of building the tabernacle?

_____

_____

_____

_____

_____

_____

_____

_____

The Church: Key Concepts

1. Read Ephesians 2:10. What has God already prepared for you?

2. Do a quick scan of the four Gospels. Did Jesus ever turn away a willing follower?

3. Read 1 Corinthians 12:4-7. Does God expect us all to serve in the same way?

_____

_____

_____

_____

_____

_____

_____

_____

_____

_____

_____

_____

_____

_____

_____

_____

_____

Thinking it through . . .

1. Do you have a habit of asking God to show you the good works He's prepared for you to do? What do you think would happen if you asked God to open your eyes to see all the opportunities before you?

2. What can God do with your willing heart, coupled with your unique gifts and abilities?

3. List at least five good works you can do this week that would mimic the loving, merciful heart of God to nonbelievers and/or help strengthen and encourage a fellow believer.

_____

_____

_____

_____

_____

_____

_____

_____

God Won't Leave You High and Dry

(EXODUS 39-40)

LIFE LESSON 39

Obedience to God brings blessings.

Some children just get it. Others seem to challenge every letter of the word *obedience*, as if they were born with omniscience and a calling to govern their flailing parents. These precious urchins have leadership skills and courage and guts. They often make confident adults, and they are the envy of shy, recluses who wish they knew how to have conversations.

However.

They are the reason hair dye exists—the kind that targets grays. They are the reason antidepressants are widely marketed. Okay, maybe I'm exaggerating. But I know lots of parents who completely understand what it's like to raise WWE impersonators who use the living room as their ring, especially when the perfect family who sits next to you at church is raising sweet Disney princesses. As one of my favorite American authors once said, "My mother had a great deal of trouble raising me, but I think she enjoyed it" (Mark Twain).

The enjoyment comes in spurts, but it's definitely NOT in the moment when your strong-willed child is accusing you of loving Thing 2 more than you love him. "You never ground him!" or "You never make him do extra chores!" or, the one that makes me want to claw my eyes out, "You love him more than me!"

As a Christian parent, I am passionate about teaching my kids that obedience to God brings blessings; disobedience leads to death and eternal separation from God. Since they are under our authority, they must practice that obedience by obeying us, their parents. When they obey, they experience our blessings—privileges, special treats, trust. When they disobey, they experience restrictions, punishments, and control.

One verse in Exodus 39 blows my mind: "According to all that the Lord had commanded Moses, so the people of Israel had done all the work" (2). For all their waywardness, they nailed this one. God gave detailed instructions for the tabernacle and all the items associated with it. This instruction manual was the size of *War and Peace*, and that was just the section written in Hebrew. Yet, God's people followed it to the letter.

Human nature probably tempted them to take short cuts—to make curtains out of cheaper material or to use gold coating instead of solid gold, to change the dimensions of the ark of the covenant so it wasn't so darn heavy. But they had glimpsed God's wrath. They caught wind that Moses had to settle God down and talk Him out of lighting a match to them all. God wasn't playing. He meant business.

So they obeyed. Maybe their hearts were pure, or maybe—like a prodigal child who's just been told he can go to the mall if he completes his list of chores—they were motivated out of fear that God would wash His hands of them even after giving them another chance. Either way, they followed e-v-e-r-y-s-i-n-g-l-e specification of God's plan.

And this time, God didn't need convincing. In fact, it seems Moses is a bit shocked at their utter compliance. Three times in verses 42 and 43, he records that they did it right. It sounds like he's amazed and incredulous, even as he pens the Holy Scripture. Holy cow—oops, not the cow again—*I can't believe this. They did it! They obeyed every word of God. They did it!*

There was only one way for Moses to respond to this kind of obedience. So he blessed them.

The Nation of Israel: Key Concepts

Read Exodus 39 as you identify these key concepts.

1. As you read the chapter, how many times do you see the phrase "as the Lord had commanded" or "as the Lord had commanded Moses"?

2. Why were the names of the sons of Israel placed on the shoulder pieces? (See Exodus 39:7.)

3. Copy Exodus 39:43. What did the Israelites do? What did Moses do?

_____

_____

_____

_____

_____

_____

_____

_____

Thinking it through . . .

1. Do you think it was hard for the people of Israel to be this obedient? Why or why not?

2. Why do you think God wanted to remember them?

3. What motivated them to obey? Do you think they knew ahead of time that they would be blessed for their obedience?

_____

_____

_____

_____

_____

_____

_____

_____

The Church: Key Concepts

1. Read Romans 6:15-23. What is the heading of this section in your Bible?

2. What choice do we have with regard to obedience? (See Romans 6:16.)

3. What is the result of obedience to sin? What is the result of the obedience to God? (See Romans 6:16, 23.)

_____

_____

_____

_____

_____

_____

_____

_____

_____

_____

_____

_____

_____

_____

_____

_____

Thinking it through . . .

1. Do you find yourself making choices out of deliberate obedience to God, or do you make choices based on what seems generally accepted by society as morally right? What is the difference between those two mentalities?

2. Do you struggle to believe the truth from Romans 6:16? Why or why not?

3. In what ways do we tend to obey the gods of our culture instead of our Creator God? How can we change this in ourselves?

_____

_____

_____

_____

_____

_____

_____

LIFE LESSON 40
Here's your sign.

I remember the first time I ever flew by myself. I was 14, and I had just finished a mission trip in Little Havana of Miami. My team flew together back to New York; then, we split to fly to our homes all across the U.S. Though I had flown many times throughout my childhood, flying by myself—especially out of such a busy airport—was unnerving.

But I was on a spiritual high, so I embraced another opportunity to trust God. As soon as I hugged my teammates goodbye, my mother's words started playing in my head.

"Find your gate first. Read the signs. Follow the directions. Ask for help if you need it." I breathed in a prayer and set out for my gate in the loud, busy terminal. A Buddhist monk, fully robed, passed me, as did a group of teenagers dressed in black. Nobody noticed me, nor would they notice if I got lost, missed my plane, or collapsed in tears.

Read the signs. Follow the directions. Incidentally, this task required me to keep my head up, a posture my parents always insisted upon anyway. As they still are, concourse and gate markers were hung from the ceiling. I gripped my paper ticket, printed on a dot matrix probably used when dinosaurs were applying for passports, and kept my eyes up.

After four weeks of prayer, worship, service, and fellowship with the Cuban refugees of Little Havana, I was almost disappointed that I found my gate so easily. My faith was strong at that moment. I was hoping for another story of amazing faith and God's provision . . . I admit, I am a bit of a drama queen. I envisioned bringing the gospel to a bathroom full of tired travelers while I waited out a canceled flight or rescuing a lost child who had been separated from his mommy in transit! But in a mundane, timely fashion, I found my gate and a seat beside it to wait in until boarding time.

I have my precious mother to thank for such an uneventful airport experience. She ingrained in me directions for where to look when I was traveling. To this day, I find myself teaching my own kids the same lesson when we are traveling: Read the signs. Follow the directions.

After the magnificent tabernacle was completed and erected as God had commanded, God gave His children similar training. They could look up and always see God's sign—a cloud during the day and a fire at night. In fact, He would move the cloud when it was time for them to pack up and journey on again. As long as they kept their eyes on His signs, they would know where to go.

Read His signs. Follow His directions. He is with you as you journey on.

The Nation of Israel: Key Concepts

Read Exodus 40 as you identify these key concepts.

1. Read the last sentence of Exodus 40:33. What did Moses do before God's presence set in over the tabernacle?

2. Read Exodus 40:35. Why was Moses not able to enter the tabernacle?

3. Read Exodus 40:36-37. What were the signs God gave the people of Israel?

_____

_____

_____

_____

_____

_____

_____

_____

Thinking it through . . .

1. What do you think is the significance of Moses's finishing the work of the tabernacle before God set up His presence among them?

2. Does it surprise you that Moses was not able to go into the tabernacle?

3. Why do you think God chose a cloud and fire as His signs?

_____

_____

_____

_____

_____

_____

_____

The Church: Key Concepts

1. What work must we finish so that Christ may dwell in us? (See Acts 16:30-33.)
2. What did Jesus promise about His presence with us? (See Matthew 28:19-20.)

_____

_____

_____

_____

_____

_____

_____

_____

_____

_____

_____

_____

_____

_____

_____

_____

Thinking it through . . .

1. Have you confessed Christ as the Son of God, repented of your sins, and been buried with Him in baptism? If so, what does it mean to you that Christ dwells within you? If not, are you ready to be obedient?

2. Does your faith reflect the truth that God is with you at all times? In other words, do you believe that He is always present with you? How does that affect your faith?

3. What are signs that God gives us to follow as we journey on with Him today?

_____

_____

_____

_____

_____

_____

_____

_____

_____

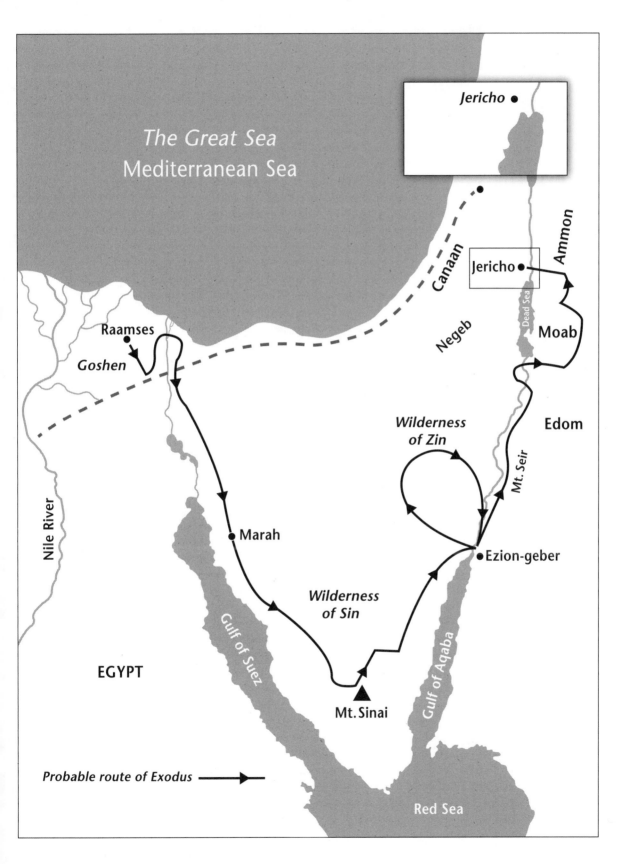

The Great Sea
Mediterranean Sea

Jericho •

Jericho •

Canaan

Ammon

Raamses •
Goshen

Negeb

Dead Sea

Moab

Wilderness of Zin

Edom

Mt. Seir

Nile River

• Marah

Ezion-geber

Wilderness of Sin

Gulf of Suez

Gulf of Aqaba

EGYPT

▲
Mt. Sinai

Probable route of Exodus ⟶

Red Sea

175